In Search of the Unusual
in
East Yorkshire
and
The Yorkshire Coast

By
Eileen Rennison

Hutton Press
1997

Published by
The Hutton Press Ltd.,
130 Canada Drive, Cherry Burton, Beverley.
East Yorkshire HU17 7SB

Copyright © 1997

Printed by
Burstwick Print & Publicity Services
13a Anlaby Road, Hull. HU1 2PJ

ISBN 1 872167 92 6

Contents

	Page
Acknowledgements.	5
Introduction.	6
1. Barmston.	7
2. Beverley.	8
3. Bishop Burton.	11
4. Bishop Wilton.	12
5. Boynton.	13
6. Bridlington.	14
7. Burton Agnes.	16
8. Carnaby.	17
9. Driffield.	18
10. Easington.	19
11. Filey.	20
12. Flamborough.	21
13. Fridaythorpe.	23
14. Garrowby.	24
15. Garton on the Wolds.	25
16. Goodmanham.	26
17. Harpham.	27
18. Hedon.	28
19. High Hawsker.	29

	Page
20. Holme on Spalding Moor.	30
21. Hornsea.	32
22. Hunmanby.	33
23. Keyingham.	34
24. Kilham.	35
25. Kilnsea.	37
26. Kingston upon Hull.	38
27. Kirby Grindalythe.	41
28. Langtoft.	42
29. Langton.	43
30. Lowthorpe.	44
31. Lund.	45
32. Lythe.	46
33. Market Weighton.	47
34. Melbourne.	48
35. Millington.	49
36. North Grimston.	50
37. Pocklington.	51
38. Redcar.	53
39. Robin Hood's Bay.	54
40. Rudston.	55

Contents (Cont.)

Page

41. Saltburn. 56
42. Scarborough. 57
43. Seaton Ross. 59
44. Settrington. 60
45. Sledmere. 61
46. Sleights. 62
47. Stamford Bridge. 63
48. Swine. 64

Page

49. Upleatham. 65
50. Warter. 66
51. Weaverthorpe. 67
52. Welton. 68
53. Whitby. 68
54. Withernsea. 71
55. Wold Newton. 72

ACKNOWLEDGEMENTS

The following works have been consulted in compiling this book:-

Churches of the Yorkshire Wolds by Christine R. Barker pub. 1985. Hutton Press.
The East Yorkshire Village Book. pub. 1991 by Countryside Books, Newbury and East Yorkshire Federation of the Women's Institute.
Yorkshire Churches by Frank Bottomley. pub. 1993 by Alan Sutton Publishing Ltd. Stroud.
Yorkshire; York and the East Riding by Nikolas Pevsner pub. 1972 Penguin Books Ltd.
Yorkshire Villages by G. Bernard Wood pub. 1971 Robert Hale, London.
Walking the Wolds by Charlie Emett pub. 1993 Cicerone Press.

My thanks are due to:-

Mr. and Mrs. Guy Stevenson for information about Kiplingcotes Derby.
Mr. Steve Goodhand and Hull Transport Museum for the photograph of Lady Chesterfield's Sleigh and for my own photographs.
Mr. K. T. Watson for the photograph and information about the Sound Mirror at Kilnsea.
Brian and Jenny Cottingham of Ye Olde White Harte, Hull.
Skelton's Bakery, Hull.
The Zetland Museum, Redcar.
and all those people whose properties are pictured and featured, making this book possible.

INTRODUCTION

The Yorkshire coast with its rugged cliffs and golden sands, sheltered coves and jutting headlands, its quaint fishing villages and resort towns is a popular source of pleasure for many people. East Yorkshire with its farmlands and rolling hills of the Wolds, its friendly villages and market towns, though not perhaps as well appreciated as it deserves, has also much to offer. Both abound in beautiful landscapes and historical associations.

This book, however, is not about the more obvious attractions of these areas. Encouraged by the reception of my first book, "In search of the unusual, in Ryedale and the North York Moors", I have set out once again to direct attention to those little, interesting and unusual items - curious buildings, odd memorials and inscriptions, follies and other strange objects, - which might otherwise be overlooked. This area of East Yorkshire being particularly rich in interesting churches, many of my unusual items are to be found in them. Sadly, because of theft, more and more churches are being kept locked, but information in the book regarding access, based on my own visits, was correct at the time of writing.

For the purpose of my book I have taken the Yorkshire coast in its entirety, down from the Tees to the Humber, not restricting myself only to the shoreline alone, but embracing the flatlands of Holderness and along the estuary to include the city of Hull. The reader will also find that I have included market towns and villages which cannot strictly be said to be on the Wolds, but which are nevertheless intimately bound to them socially and commercially. I hope that I may be excused if I have strayed and stretched a point here and there, and that the contents of the book will interest, surprise, inform and amuse the reader and encourage him or her to explore further. It would be impossible to include all the places and items of interest in this area so full of history, in one small book, even if time permitted one to seek them all out. I make no claim to have done so. Some of the items were already familiar to me but many were delightful surprises discovered when researching something else. If I have overlooked anyone's favourite place I hope that they will understand and that others will find as much pleasure in the search for the unusual as I have.

Directions to each place of interest are given; for ease and simplicity these are routed along main roads but readers may like to turn off and plan their own routes to enjoy the pleasure of driving on the many relatively traffic free minor roads in the area.

Places are arranged in alphabetical order but with a little study of a map it will be seen that visits to more than one may be included in one outing, though some may be felt worthy of a special visit on their own.

Eileen Rennison
York, 1997.

1. BARMSTON

Barmston is on the coast south of Bridlington and north of Hornsea. From Bridlington take the A165 for about 5½ miles, then turn left to Barmston a further ¾ mile.

From Hornsea take the B1242 for about 8 miles, turn right onto the A165 before turning right again to Barmston after about ¾ mile.

Park in the village. Take the public footpath down Chapel lane (near the pub), cross the stile and follow the path across the field; follow the front edge of the wood to the righthand corner of the field then the path across the end of the wood.

'Woodhenge'.

Barmston is not on the road to anywhere else, but the traveller on the way to Bridlington or Hornsea would do well to make a small diversion to see a strange and dramatic memorial there. Immediately on entering the village it can be seen in the distance across the fields to the right, on a small hill, starkly silhouetted against the sky. It has an eerie and intriguing air about it that calls out for a closer view. 'Woodhenge' as it has been dubbed was erected by Mr. Chris. Marshall, the owner of farms and land in the area. Now living in New Zealand he only visits his estate at intervals but has left his mark on the landscape in the form of a sort of memorial to death. Trusey Hill where it stands is thought to have been the site of an ancient monastery and under the group

of dead tree trunks preserved and transplanted there, lie a skeleton found on the site, a gun carriage of Great War vintage washed up on the beach, and other items.

I am told that the villagers were originally not too happy about its erection. It is certainly very strange, but for my part, I found it a wonderful, impressive and evocative sight.

'Woodhenge'.
Photo by Eileen Rennison.

2. BEVERLEY

From Hull take the A1079 out to join the A1174 to Beverley about 7 miles.
From Driffield Beverley is about 12 miles on the A164.

From York take the A1079 past Market Weighton and beyond Bishop Burton until it joins the A1035 into Beverley - about 30 miles.

There are car parks centrally placed in the town and the items mentioned are within reasonable walking distances. The Minster is well signposted.

The Largest Parish Church in England.

Because of its size and impressive appearance Beverley Minster is often mistaken for a cathedral, its title, too, confusing those who believe minster and cathedral to be synonymous terms. It is however a parish church, dedicated to St. John the Evangelist and St. Martin, its origins said to go back to the Christian settlement founded there in the 8th century by St. John of Beverley. His remains lie in a vault under a commemorative slab in the east end of the Nave. In the Choir an ancient and unusual item, of which there are only two other examples can be seen. The so-called Frid or Frith Chair dates back to Saxon times and is thought originally to have been a bishop's chair, until 937 when the Minster was granted the Right of Sanctuary and that cold stone chair became the Sanctuary Chair. Under the Right a fugitive from the law who reached Sanctuary was housed for thirty days while the case against him was looked into and depending on the verdict escorted safely

'Beverley Minster'.
Photo by Eileen Rennison.

Beverley Minster 'Frid' or 'Frith' chair.
Photo by Eileen Rennison.

out of the county or to the coast to enable him to leave the country. Some visitors may be surprised to find in the church so many items of an amusing and humorous nature. The miserichords in the Choir stalls (small hinged seats to provide rests during lengthy periods of worship) have a variety of interesting carvings decorating their undersides, some of which are bound to raise a smile. The North Aisle contains carvings of musicians playing medieval instruments said to be the largest collection of such instruments in the world. More strange perhaps are the carvings there which depict such painful ailments as lumbago, sciatica, toothache and stomachache! In the Central Aisle of the Nave are carvings of musical angels, whose playing appears to be unappreciated by others with fingers in their ears!

Minstrels, Kings, and a Rabbit.

Having seen the misericords and the carved musicians with their medieval instruments in the Minster the visitor should not fail to take the opportunity to compare them with similar ones in St. Mary's church. From the Minster proceed along Eastgate or Highgate into the Wednesday Market then through to Toll Gavel, making sure to notice there the doorway of number 44, once a chemist's shop and adorned with wrought iron snakes, the symbol of Resculapius, the God of Medicine, then cross the Saturday Market to St. Mary's at the junction of Hengate and North Bar Within. This church, dating from the 12th century is of such magnificence as to be often mistaken for the Minster. Like the Minster its carvings show a concern with musicians. Beverley was a chief centre in the North for the Guild of Musicians and in

No. 44 Toll Gavel.
Photo by
Eileen Rennison.

1524 as a tribute to their contribution to the building of this part of the church, a pier in the North Arcade of the Nave has a splendid carving of the Minstrels of Beverley with their instruments - pipes, tabor, viol, bombard, cittern, and hautboy, - the central figure being the president of the Guild proudly wearing his badge of office. The painted ceiling of the Chancel is a remarkable record of the Kings of England from 1445. It was repaired and repainted in the 19th century and cleaned in 1939, when I believe that George the Fifth was added, though I was not able to identify him. In the North Choir Aisle at the doorway to the sacristy is a carving of a small rabbit, which is claimed to have been the inspiration for the White Rabbit in Lewis Carroll's *Alice in Wonderland*. Certainly he was familiar with this

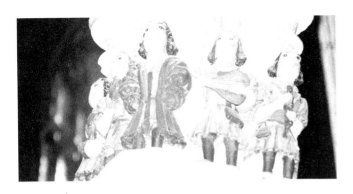

St. Mary's Church minstrels.
Photo by Richard Hebblethwaite.

eastern part of the country. His grandfather was a customs officer at Hull and his father Rector of Croft just over the Humber. He was know to have visited Beverley and it is quite possible that the white stone rabbit in St. Mary's caught his eye, to be remembered and transformed at a later date into the anxious scurrying character depicted by Tenniel in his drawings for Carroll's much-loved book. It is nice to think so, anyway!

St. Mary's Church ceiling.
Photo by Richard Hebblethwaite.

Political Carving.

North Bar is the only remaining medieval gateway into Beverley and gives its name to the streets either side of it, North Bar Within and North Bar Without. In 1850 James Edward Elwell came from Birmingham to set up a thriving business as a cabinet maker and woodcarver at 4 North Bar Without. His artist son Fred Elwell later achieved recognition as a Royal Academician and found inspiration for his paintings throughout his lifetime on Beverley and its people. The organ screen in Beverley Minster is James Elwell's great work but many examples are still to be seen in or on Victorian buildings in the town. An amusing and unusual work of his is a carving in the form of a political cartoon, unexpectedly situated above the door of number 4 North Bar Without. Beautifully executed, it shows Disraeli on a covered wagon displaying his 'wares' to a gullible electorate, under the title of The Political Cheap Jack.

'Political carving'.
Photo by Richard Hebblethwaite.

3. BISHOP BURTON

John Wesley in the Church.

Bishop Burton is on the A1079 road about 27½ miles from York and 2½ miles from Beverley. Turn up the left side of the pond and the church is behind it. There is parking space beside the church, through the lich-gate, up a very steep hill.

Bishop Burton is a lovely picture-postcard village, with ducks on the pond, attractive white cottages and a village green. There John Wesley (1703-1791) the founder of Methodism, once preached, as was his practice, in the open air, under a great wych-elm. It seems appropriate that when the huge hollow tree was blown down in a storm in January 1836, a bust of Wesley should have been carved out of wood from the tree.

The splendid bust that was created can still be seen in Bishop Burton, though not as one might expect in the Methodist church. It seems that the Methodists for some reason wanted to dispose of the bust. A vicar of All Saints Church bought it and now Wesley, with hands upraised as if in blessing, looks down from the south wall of the church, on a Church of England congregation. An unusual and unexpected place to find him perhaps, but we should remember that he was, after all, the son of a rector and himself a member of the Church of England.

There are other items of interest in the church. The Chancel contains some fine brasses and in the Nave is a curious and somewhat macabre 17th century monument to Rachel and Elizabeth Gee. Rachel lies wrapped in a winding sheet, with the infant Elizabeth, wearing bonnet and dress standing by her head. The pew-ends of Austrian oak are decorated with the figures of saints, carved in Bruges. When I visited the church was locked but was opened on application to the house beside the gate.

John Wesley in the church.
Photo by Richard Hebblethwaite.

4. BISHOP WILTON

The Vatican design in a village church.

From Stamford Bridge - 5 miles along the A166 road to Bridlington at the foot of Garrowby Hill turn right to Bishop Wilton, about 1 mile. In the village turn left alongside the green. About 100 yards, opposite some steps down to the green is the iron gateway to the church.

From Pocklington - Take the road out to Bishop Wilton turning left after about 1 mile out to Meltonby approximately 2½ miles, then right to Bishop Wilton. In the village turn right along the left hand side of the green to the gateway to the church.

The village of Bishop Wilton is attractive and unusual with its hollow moat-like green, a trickle of water running through it at one point. Archbishop Grey of York (1216 to 1255) built himself a palace in the village of Wilton thus giving it the present name of Bishop Wilton.

The 120 foot high spire of St. Edith's church, one of the so-called 'Sykes churches of the Wolds', rises behind the houses alongside the village green. Sir Tatton Sykes of Sledmere was instrumental in the restoration of many churches in the 19th century, the church at Bishop Wilton being one which he rescued from a ruinous state. A window and bust to his memory can be seen in the church.

But perhaps the most splendid and unusual feature to be seen there is a black and white marble mosaic floor, the design of birds by Salviati copied from a floor in the Vatican which in turn originated in the palace of the Caesars of Rome. The beautiful painted roof decorated with colours and gold leaf is also impressive, as is the font, richly carved with figures of saints, and its elaborate cover, depicting the four Evangelists Matthew, Mark, Luke and John, and between them St. Gregory, St. Augustine, St. Jerome and St. Ambrose, the four doctor saints.

The Vatican design in the village church.
Photo by Eileen Rennison.

5. BOYNTON

Turkey Lectern.

From the outskirts of Bridlington take the A165 north for about ¹/₂ mile then left onto the B1253 for about 2 miles. Turn left into South Boynton.

From Sledmere the village, which is divided into north and south by the B1253, is about 11¹/₂ miles. Turn right into South Boynton.

St. Andrew's church is tucked in close to the Hall gateway in South Boynton. Its exterior architecture appears unexceptional and does not prepare one for the interior. A leaflet in the church describes it as 'a study in green'; an apt description, for the altar, all the pews and other woodwork are painted in a soft matt green. Columns supporting a gallery at the west end, and the chancel arch, give an impression of classical architecture, until one notices the capitals, which have a distinct suggestion of the Egyptian. It is altogether an interesting church, not least among its unusual features being the lectern. This is not the usual eagle, but a turkey, in commemoration of its introduction into this country by William Strickland of Boynton Hall who sailed to the New World with Sebastian Cabot, and on his return incorporated what was then an unknown and exotic bird, into his family crest. Today it has become a commonplace, but as we enjoy our Christmas turkey perhaps we might give a thought and thanks to William Strickland of Boynton. Queen Henrietta Maria stayed overnight at the Hall in 1643 after landing at Bridlington from Holland where she had been to raise money for arms to support her husband Charles I. The next day she departed to join him in York, making off with the family silver and leaving only a portrait of herself in return!

St. Andrew's church - the turkey lectern.
Photo by Eileen Rennison.

6. BRIDLINGTON

Bridlington is on the coast 16 miles south of Scarborough on the A165, or 11 miles from Driffield on the A166. Applegarth Lane is in Bridlington Old Town and can be approached from the outskirts without entering the town centre. Applegarth Lane is off to the right just past the Bayle. The tiny chapel is on the right behind iron railings. For the Lawrence memorial follow the signposting to the city centre, South Sands and the Harbour, where there is a large car park.

A street map showing one-way streets can be obtained from the Information Office in Prince Street near the Harbour.

Remembering Lawrence of Arabia.

Colonel Thomas Edward Lawrence, soldier, archaeologist and expert in Oriental languages, spent some years in Arabia, where he lived and dressed as an Arab, studying the ancient monuments and buried cities and mastering the different dialects and customs. During the Great War of 1914-18, his expertise thus gained was invaluable in organising the Arabs against the Turks, a task which earned him the name of 'Lawrence of Arabia'. After the war he sought to retire from public recognition, and enlisted in the R.A.F. under the name of T.E. Shaw. This much may be well known, if only because of the film which was made of his exploits; perhaps less well known is the fact that he spent part of his R.A.F. career as a marine craft mechanic with the Air Sea

The Lawrence of Arabia memorial.

Rescue career as a marine craft mechanic with the Air Sea Rescue at Bridlington. He was killed in a motor-cycle accident in 1935, only three months after leaving Bridlington. His presence there does not go unmarked however. In a small rest garden opposite the Harbour car park is a sundial commemorating him, appropriately close to where the workshops were, in which he worked, and where he stayed, on the corner of Windsor Crescent, in what is now the Royal Yorkshire Yacht Club

The Gypsey Race or Woe Waters.

The Gypsey Race, despite its name, has nothing to do with a Romany competition, but is one of the few streams of this chalkland area, and derives its name from the Norse word 'gypa' meaning a spring. It rises near Duggleby and makes its way, often underground, through the Great Wold Valley to Bridlington where it runs into the harbour, passing through or near to such villages as Weaverthorpe, Burton Fleming, Wold Newton, Rudston, and Boynton, on the way. It is a strange and fascinating feature, which because of its erratic and elusive behaviour - sometimes disappearing for years at a time, only to bubble forth again - has led to its acquiring the name of Woe Waters and the superstition that when it flows some great disaster will occur. Since it is not difficult to find some disaster occurring somewhere at any given time, no doubt believers have been able to point to the 'truth' of it over the years! A more scientific view is that the porous nature of chalk and the height of the water table are involved. Beside the harbour car park at Bridlington the Gypsey Race ends its mysterious journey to emerge from beneath the houses into the harbour. When I visited Bridlington in March 1995 it was indeed living up to its name of Race, flowing vigorously in a little stream across the harbour into the sea. A local lady told me that they had not seen it so for a long time - though despite the superstition disasters in the world seemed no more numerous than usual to me! I was sad to see a notice nearby warning that sewage was present in the Race. It seems a sordid end for an elusive and romantic stream, after its hide-and-seek journey through the countryside.

The Gypsey Race.

Tiny Baptist Chapel.

Applegarth Lane in Bridlington Old Town was once the orchard of the Priory, of which the church and the Bayle, or gate house are the only buildings remaining. The visitor to the Bayle, now a museum, may be interested to walk a few yards down Applegarth Lane to where in 1699 a tiny chapel was built, by a Scottish farmer whose ship was forced into Bridlington Bay by a storm, as he was returning home from a journey to London on business, Only twelve feet square, with twenty original members, it was the first Baptist chapel to be established in East Yorkshire. Today, with its windows boarded up, its gate padlocked and its pathway full of weeds, it could be mistaken for a rather neglected outhouse, which seems a sad shame for what is a small but interesting relic of the area's history.

The Baptist chapel.
Photos by Eileen Rennison.

7. BURTON AGNES

A Telling Shadow in a Maze.

Burton Agnes lies on the A166 about 4³/₄ miles from Bridlington and 6 miles from Driffield. The turn in the village to the Hall, Old Manor and church is clearly marked and parking is provided opposite the Hall gateway. The Hall is open April 1 - October 31.

The village of Burton Agnes is the setting for the gem of Tudor architecture that is Burton Agnes Hall. There is much to delight the visitor there in both house and grounds. A fairly recent addition to the latter is the maze built in 1990. Its goal is a dovecote with its fluttering birds, only to be reached by trial and error in choosing the correct paths between the chest-high bushes.

At one point in the journey a clearing is reached, in which a stone slab bearing the months of the year and some numbered stones are arranged. Obeying the instructions given I stood on the part of the slab marked September, the month in which I visited. The sun shone and my shadow fell about midway between the stones twelve and one. I checked my watch. It was twenty minutes to one. Pretty accurate for a human sundial I thought - and an unusual and interesting feature.

Donkey Work.

Behind the old Manor House to the left of the Hall is an open brick building housing a large old water-wheel; a rare example of an ancient method of raising water from the well. It was worked by a donkey and turning it must surely have been a hard monotonous task for the poor beast, forever walking round within it, getting nowhere.

Tree Tunnel.

The approach to the church some 100 yds further along from the entrance to the Hall, is unusual and somewhat forbidding. Yew trees along each side of the church path have been cut and trained to meet overhead forming a neat dark green tunnel to the door. The church contains many memorials and though as old as the Manor House was much restored in the 19th century by the Archdeacon son of William Wilberforce the reformer and slavery abolitionist, who was a native of Hull.

Above:
A telling shadow in a maze.

Right:
Donkey work.

Photos by
Eileen Rennison.

8. CARNABY

East Yorkshire's Greek Temple of the Winds.

Carnaby lies on the A166 about $3^1/_4$ miles beyond Burton Agnes, approximately 10 miles from Driffield and $2^1/_2$ miles from Bridlington. The Temple is about a mile from the main road on a bridleway past Temple Farm. Park in the carpark by the public house, off the main road to the right from Driffield and left from Bridlington. From there turn left back into the main road, then right to Church Lane and School Hill, then left to Temple Lane.

In the late 18th century Sir George Strickland of Boynton Hall, whose ancestor had brought the turkey to England, built himself a folly, an idea popular with the nobility and gentry at that time. Lofty and octagonal in plan it was built of brick but otherwise inspired by the Temple of the Winds in Athens. Its two-storied height topped by a lantern gave unhindered views across the fields away towards the coast. An excellent look-out, which was no doubt the factor which led to its military use in World War Two. Today its windows are bricked up against the possibility of vandalism, and yet it is still an impressive and interesting building, which can be seen towering blind-eyed above the fields from far away.

East Yorkshire Greek Temple of the winds.
Photo by Richard Hebblethwaite.

9. DRIFFIELD

Driffield is about 25 miles from York and 5 miles from Bridlington on the A166. The Pinfold is at the northern end of the town at the foot of Moot Hill.

Capital of the Wolds.

Burials from the Bronze and Iron Ages and evidence of the Romans and Anglo-Saxons have been found in and around Driffield. A motte and bailey castle and eight watermills as well as fine churches were all recorded there in the Domesday Book. Today only earthworks remain of the castle, but after many ups and downs in its prosperity over the centuries, the town, with its industries connected to farming, can confidently proclaim itself Capital of the Wolds. The opening of the Driffield canal in 1772 brought trade and prosperity to the town, necessitating the building of large warehouses for the cargoes of grain going in one direction and coal coming in return. But traffic in the following century began to decline. The last commercial craft was in 1944, before the canal became unnavigable. Bradshaw's huge Flour Mill is a towering feature of the canal scene, but despite its size I understand that today it is worked by just three men. An echo of Driffield's early past remains in the name Moot Hill, once the meeting place of the Saxon Town Moot, an assembly which may perhaps be likened to the modern Town Council. At the foot of Moot Hill is a reminder of a later period. The medieval pinfold, where straying animals were kept until reclaimed by their owners, was restored in 1973. The visitor to the town at the beginning of the year might perhaps be lucky enough to see the strange old custom of 'scrambling', the origins of which are something of a mystery. On the first day of the New Year the children of the town work their way down the main shopping street, chanting and asking for favours. The shopkeepers in response throw out pennies and 'goodies' for them to scramble for.

A medieval pinfold.
Photo by Richard Hebblethwaite.

10. EASINGTON

Easington is about 18½ miles east of Hull, taking the A1033 for about 12½ miles then the B1445 for a further 6 miles. Turn right opposite Beck Lane and beside All Saints church, then left into South Church Side. The barn can be seen on the right.

The Only Remaining Tithe Barn in East Yorkshire.

Tithes were payments in goods to support the parish priests or the monasteries providing clergy. They consisted of one tenth of all the produce of the land in the parish, including not only crops but animals, butter, eggs, and often the profits from handicrafts and merchandise. The earliest tithes were introduced in 794 and continued in some form as late as the 19th century. Huge barns were built to store the tithes and some are almost cathedral-like with nave-and-aisle construction, giving an indication of the size and productivity of the land involved. The tithe barn at Easington dates from the 14th century and is the only one remaining in East Yorkshire. It is built of brick with a thatched roof and porch, and high wooden doors. I had heard that it now houses a folk museum but it seems that that is not so. Disappointingly when I visited (May 1995) I was unable to see inside or indeed find any way of getting close, and had to be content to view it over the fence from the street. Even so it is an interesting and unique survival of an ancient practice and well worth a visit. Future visitors may be luckier than I in making the appropriate contact in order to obtain permission to view the barn.

The only remaining tithe barn in East Yorkshire.

Photo by Eileen Rennison.

11. FILEY

Filey lies off the A165 coast road about 6 miles south of Scarborough.

Filey Brigg is to the north of the town.

St. Oswald's church is in Church Ravine. Follow the main road into town to a roundabout, go straight on into Church Cliff Drive, then turn right to the Ravine. There is parking nearby.

Nature's Pier or the Devil's Causeway.

The Devil decided to build a causeway from Filey all the way across the North Sea but soon got tired of it and abandoned the task. As he was packing up his tools he dropped his hammer into the sea, and plunging his hand in the water to retrieve it he grasped instead a fish between his thumb and finger. That, the legend would have us believe, is how Filey Brigg came about, and how the haddock, at the same time, got its distinctive markings.

It is not surprising if in ancient times such a story was thought to be the explanation of what is a quite remarkable geological curiosity, an outcrop of rock reaching out like a natural pier, about 3/4 mile to sea. It is possible at low tide to walk along the Brigg, but the currents are strong and the breakers can be fierce. A wary eye should always be kept on the weather and the tides. Anglers have been known to be engulfed and washed away and ships wrecked on the rocks. The Brigg is said to take its name from the Scandinavian word for a landing place, though it is in fact a place for ships to avoid because of its dangers.

On the cliff above the Brigg one of several signal stations established along this stretch of coast stood to give warning of invasion in Roman times.

A Boy Bishop.

The church of St. Oswald at Filey is appropriately dedicated to the patron saint of fishermen. A window in the church dating from 1885 and known as the Fishermen's Window, remembers the local men lost at sea whose bodies were never recovered. Next to it is a memorial from a very much earlier date, reminding us of a strange old ceremony, discontinued as sacrilegious, after the Reformation. A Boy Bishop was elected in large parishes, from the choir or grammar school, to be the principal figure in certain church revels of the Middle Ages. From December 6th, the day of St. Nicholas, patron saint of children, until Holy Innocent's Day on December 28th, the chosen boy was invested with the full insignia of a bishop and presided over the church services, and was responsible for the behaviour of boys dressed as priests. The memorial in St. Oswald's church is dated between 1250 and 1300. It seems that the Boy Bishop who is commemorated must have died in office.

Above:
A boy bishop.

Right:
Filey Brigg.

Photos by Richard Hebblethwaite.

12. FLAMBOROUGH

Flamborough is about 4 miles east of Bridlington on the B1255. St. Oswald's church is on the right shortly after entering the village. It is not possible to park immediately in front of the church. Flamborough Head and Lighthouses are about 2 miles beyond on the B1259. There is pay-and-display parking near the lighthouses.

Medieval Rood Loft.

The word 'rood' is the old name for a cross or crucifix; in particular for the great crucifix on the screen dividing the Chancel from the Nave in English churches. Many, from the 14th century to the Reformation, also had a gallery or rood loft, which ran along the top, and from which parts of the service were recited or sung. At the Reformation these rood lofts were among the many church features that were destroyed. Only two survived in Yorkshire. One of them is to be seen in St. Oswald's church in Flamborough. The other is in Hubberholme church in the Yorkshire Dales. The loft at Flamborough consists of richly carved panels and canopies though the figures once adorning it have disappeared. St. Oswald's church contains other unusual items of interest. On one wall is a replica of a royal pardon granted to Walter Strickland by Charles II in 1660, absolving him from a charge of treason, despite his long association with Charles's enemies.

Beside the Altar is the tomb of Sir Marmaduke Constable, surmounted by the rib-cage of a skeleton containing the heart and an odd stone said to depict the toad, which legend would have us believe ate away his heart and caused his death in 1530, after being accidentally swallowed in a drink of water. The church is presently (at the time of my visit May 1995) only open in school holiday times, from 10 am to 3 pm.

A medieval rood loft.
Photo by Eileen Rennison.

Lights Past and Present.

In 1674 Sir John Clayton built what is acknowledged to be the oldest remaining lighthouse in England, the Chalk Tower on Flamborough Head. The warning beacon was simply a coal fire in a cresset on top of the octagonal tower. Sir John sought to pay for it by means of a toll from passing ships. The scheme, not surprisingly, was not very successful. The tolls, which must surely have been difficult to enforce and collect, proved insufficient for its upkeep. In 1806, Trinity House, the maritime corporation founded in 1514 for the purpose of supervising all lighthouses and beacons and the charting of wrecks and dangers, became convinced of the necessity for a proper, more efficient lighthouse on Flamborough Head. The present lighthouse was built, nearer the sea, without the use of scaffolding by John Matson of Bridlington. It was finished and operating within five months. The lantern at the top of the 92 feet high tower was lit by oil and revolved by clockwork until modernised with electronics in 1985. Its flashing light can be seen 21 miles out to sea.

Photos by Eileen Rennison.

13. FRIDAYTHORPE

'Time is Short, Eternity is Long.'

Fridaythorpe is about 16 miles from Bridlington on the A166, or 10½ miles beyond Stamford Bridge on the same road from York to Bridlington. On entering the village from the Bridlington direction take a right turn across the front of the Manor House Inn.

The church lychgate is about 200 yards, just past the pond on the right. Or, a little further on take the first turn right to arrive at a small side gate. Turn left at the Manor House Inn if approaching from York direction.

In the highest village on the Wolds, the good people of Fridaythorpe go about their industrious everyday life reminded by the melodious chimes of the church clock that "Time is short, Eternity is long.' That is the inscription on the unusual clock-face on the squat tower of St. Mary's church. Made of wood, decorated with black and white scroll work, it is a copy of one in an 18th century French chateau, and may seem somewhat incongruous on this small Norman church, but its very disproportion and unexpectedness add a charm of their own.

Inside the interesting interior of the church is a mystery. Carved on a column are the words, 'This 713 found here'. What can it mean? Does anyone know, I wonder?

A word of warning immediately on opening the church door there are steps down, and the interior was very dark when I visited.

St. Mary's church.
Photo by Eileen Rennison.

14. GARROWBY

Latin Bells.

From Stamford Bridge take the A166 up Garrowby Hill. The bells are on the right hand side of the road and on minor roads off.

About 9 miles out of Stamford Bridge, travelling along the A166, one may be puzzled by several bell-shaped stones to be seen in gaps in the hedges on the righthand side, just beyond the top of Garrowby. On further investigation they are shown to have inscriptions in Latin, but the fact that they are of concrete rather than stone gives the clue that they are not, as one might have supposed, ancient relics from this area's rich Roman past, though that must surely have been their inspiration.

I missed out on Latin at school and so have had to rely on others to decipher their messages. They appear to be descriptive of the fields or their situation. One pair on the main road is inscribed EBORACUM and VIA XX which seems to translate as Road to York with the figures perhaps being the miles from York. Another pair - ACER ARVUM could perhaps suggest arable land of vigorous growth, and yet another pair - LARGUS LINGUA - a bountiful 'tongue' of land. Down the side-road to Millington two more pairs can be seen at a minor crossroad. LIMES -TRAMES, I am told mean boundary path and side path respectively and VIRIDIA -VIA ISTAC something like trees by the road that way. There are several more in the vicinity than the ones mentioned here, placed there in the 1960s by a farmer from Wold House Farm to mark , in his own idiosyncratic way, the boundaries of his land.

An unusual and intriguing way of doing it.

Latin Bells.
Photos by
Eileen Rennison.

15. GARTON-ON-THE-WOLDS

A Church in the Decorated Style.

Garton-on-the-Wolds is on the A166 about 3 miles from Driffield and 17½ miles from Stamford Bridge. In the village the church is off the main road to the left from the Driffield end, to the right from Stamford Bridge.

The church of St. Michael and All Angels at Garton-on-the-Wolds has many Norman features and is one of the many Wolds churches restored in the 19th century by the two Sir Tatton Sykes of Sledmere. Yet in one sense it can only best be described as a decorated church!

Its exterior gives no hint of what one is to see inside. On first entering the interior is rather dark, but a notice helps one locate the light switches, and when the lights go on one is met by a sight so rich as to make one's jaw drop. Every available area of both wall and ceiling is covered with coloured tiles, paintings and decoration; the floor is a mosaic of black and white and yellow. The paintings are in imitation of 13th century frescos though clearly suggesting the Victorian period in which they were done. More recently the church was chosen and the restoration of the murals was carried out in commemoration of Sir Nikolaus Pevsner the architectural historian who died in 1983. The colourful paintings of saints and scenes from the Bible are too numerous to be described here. They are something one should not fail to go and see for oneself.

In passing look out along the main street of the village for the beautifully detailed cockerel roosting outside the blacksmith's shop, its feathers made from metal strips and its claws firmly gripping the railing.

Above:
A golden cockerel.
Photo by
Richard Hebblethwaite.

Right:
A church in the
decorated style.
Photo by
Eileen Rennison.

16. GOODMANHAM

A Temple Destroyed.

From York take the A1079 for about 18½ miles to Market Weighton. Turn left in the main street to road signposted to Goodmanham, then turn right on the outskirts opposite the Black Horse inn to Goodmanham 1 mile. Continue through the village to the church on the left. The key can be obtained from Rectory Farm opposite or the Goodmanham Arms.

From Beverley take the A1035 for about 2 miles then the A1079 for about 7½ miles to Market Weighton, turning right there, then as above.

Goodmanham today gives no hint of the dramatic scene and important historic event which took place there in AD627. Goodmundingham, as it was then called, was the centre for pagan religion in the north of England with a temple dedicated to the god Woden. Its High Priest, Coifi, was a frequent visitor and religious adviser to King Edwin of Northumbria, at his summer palace at nearby Londesborough. Edwin's Queen Ethelburga was a Christian and sought to convert her husband. When she brought the missionary Paulinus, who later became the first prelate of York, to Londesborough in AD 627, to preach the word at the Great Council of Northumbria, surprisingly, Coifi was amongst the first to be convinced of the truth of Christianity. He advised the king to destroy the pagan temple but no one dared risk the wrath of the gods in doing so. It was Coifi himself who finally took his spear and set about destroying the idols. When he remained unscathed, others took courage and completed the destruction, setting fire to the temple. Appropriately, this episode of English history is recorded in a stained glass window in the Nave of the church at Goodmanham, which is said to be built on the site of that ancient temple. Other items of interest in the church include what is said to be the most elaborately carved font in East Yorkshire and also in contrast a plain tub font of great age which was for may years used as a farmyard drinking trough, unrecognised for what it was. The curious monument showing only head and feet is reputed to be that of a long forgotten monk guilty of some serious misdemeanour. I find this hard to believe. Surely such a monk would hardly be commemorated? And the head does not look at all like a monk. I can't help thinking that I have been given the wrong story, but it is nevertheless an intriguing monument.

Right:
A temple destroyed.

Below:
A plain tub font.

Photos by
Richard Hebblethwaite.

17. HARPHAM

Two Wells and Legends.

From Bridlington on the A166 after about 7 miles turn left and continue for a further 1 mile.
From Driffield on the A166 turn right after about 4¹/₂ miles and continue for 1 mile.
St. John's Well - continue the full length of the village main street, past a farm with blue painted iron railings into a dead-end lane. The well is on the right just before a field gate.
Drummer's Well - Turn right in the main village street to the church and take the public footpath beside it. The well is to the left beyond the tennis courts in the pasture south of the church.

Harpham is a village with two wells and some interesting folklore. In the field to the south of the church, where once the manor of Harpham stood, is the well known as Drummer's Well. There are versions with slight variations of detail, but the legend attached to it says that the lord of the manor St. Quintin, and nobles, were holding a field day with archery when St. Quintin, with a sudden movement, accidentally knocked his drummer boy Tom Hewson into the well, where despite valiant efforts to save him he drowned. His mother, the wise woman of the village, on hearing the news, rushed to the scene and declared that from that day on the sound of drumming from the well would precede and foretell the death of any member of the St. Quintin family. This story is said to date from as long ago as the 1300s.

The second well, named after St. John of Beverley, who it is claimed was born in the village in 640AD (although Cherry Burton village also lays claim to that honour) can be found at the eastern end of the village. St. John's tomb, in Beverley minster which he founded, is decorated every Spring with primroses gathered in the local woods by the children of Harpham. On the nearest Tuesday evening to St John's Day on the 7th of May, I understand that the choirboys from Beverley Minster process from the church in Harpham to the decorated well, but sadly when I visited Harpham on May 10th 1994 I saw no sign of this ceremony. Perhaps I chose the wrong Tuesday, or the wrong time.

The legend of the well is that when a retreating army arrived in the village exhausted and urgently needing water, St. John struck his staff on the ground bringing forth the pure water which has never since ceased to flow.

St. John's well.
Photo by
Eileen Rennison.

18. HEDON

From Hull take the A1033 for about 4 miles then the B1362 into Hedon.

From Withernsea Hedon is about 10 miles on the B1362. From Beverley, after about 4½ miles on the A1035 turn right onto the A165 to Skirlaugh; after 6½ miles turn left about ½ mile after Coniston to Bilton a further 1½ miles and join the B1239 to Preston 2 miles, then take the B1240 to Hedon.

In Hedon follow the one-way signs into Baxtergate. Holyrood House is on the corner of Baxtergate and Magdalen Lane.

The Bolingbroke Cross.

The busy small town of Hedon is steeped in history. Once more important than Hull, in the 12th century it was the major port of the Humber. Its great church of St. Augustine is known as the King of Holderness, the counterpart to the Queen of Holderness church at Patrington. The civic mace of Hedon, engraved with the coats of arms of both England and France was made in the reign of Henry V (1413 - 1422) and is claimed to be the oldest in the country. And, tucked away in a quiet garden behind Holyrood House is a cross, twenty feet high with a weathered and eroded heraldic device on top, known as the Bolingbroke Cross. It once marked the spot where Henry Bolingbroke landed to claim the throne of England. In 1398 Henry, son of John of Gaunt Duke of Lancaster, grandson of Edward III and

Cousin of Richard II, was sent into exile for opposing Richard. When his father died in 1399 Henry returned ostensibly to claim his estates, but in reality to depose Richard and set himself upon the throne. He landed at Ravenser on the coast, a place which was later washed away and lost to erosion. The cross which was also lost was washed up in 1818 at Kilnsea and moved to Hedon for safety from the problems of land erosion. The garden in which the cross stands is accessible through an open archway in Magdalen Lane, but it must be remembered that Holyrood House is a Care Home and one should be careful not to intrude.

The Bolingbroke cross.

Photo by Eileen Rennison.

19. HIGH HAWSKER

Boiling Well.

From Whitby take the A171 south for 3 miles then turn left on to the B1447 and into the village. The well is about 1 mile beyond the village at the roadside on the left.

The dialect verse

"Lang centuries back,
This wor t'owld Abbey well.
St. Hilda veiled in black
Supped fra it an' found nay lack.'

associates this well, like the one in the churchyard at Hinderwell, with St. Hilda the 7th century Abbess who founded Whitby Abbey. The modern tablet on the front of the small brick structure that covers it, states simply however that the spring 'served the local community from the 12th century.' The further information that 'in the early 19th century its waters were carted to a reservoir at Whitby Abbey then piped to Whitby houses east of the Esk' suggests the possibility that the connection with St. Hilda may have originated as recently as that time only, because of the connection with the Abbey. The rather strange name Boiling Well I take to be a reference to its seething emission and not to its temperature. The spring obviously still produces an abundant supply of water, as due to the boggy state of the ground behind it I was unable to get more than a glimpse into the dark, wet interior through the open door at the back. The plain little brick structure has a very

nondescript air about it, but that only seems to add to the sense of amazement that it should have once been the water supply for a community for so long, and the fact of water from so humble a source actually being carted to a distance to supply Whitby houses is almost beyond our present-day imagination.

Boiling Well.
Photo by Eileen Rennison.

20. HOLME-UPON-SPALDING MOOR

From Hull or Beverley follow the A1079 for approximately 20 miles through Bishop Burton, skirting Market Weighton, until just before Shiptonthorpe taking a left turn onto the A163 to Holme-Upon-Spalding Moor, a further 5 miles.

The entry to the road to the church is on the left immediately after a petrol station and needs a sharp eye not to miss it. Continue straight ahead for Workhouse Farm then take the A614 road to Howden for about a mile. The farm is at the roadside on the left.

Up On The Hill ...

The church at Holme-upon-Spalding Moor can be seen long before the village is reached. High upon a hill it is in a unique and commanding position, though the steepness of its winding road must present difficulties of access to its parishioners in bad weather. Unfortunately the church is locked with no indication of where one may obtain the key, but making up for this disappointment, the view from the top of the hill is surely one of the most spectacular in the county. Standing by the lychgate one can see for miles around across a panoramic stretch of countryside.

The lychgate itself is a memorial to the dead of two World Wars. The commemoration includes those member of the R.A.F. and the Australian Air force who were stationed nearby during World War Two and are now buried in the churchyard. Above the gate at the front the words *Mors Janua Vitae* (Death the Key to Life) are carved and on the other side the lovely words 'Till the morning break and the shadows flee away.' An unusual, very large and colourfully decorated crucifix dominates the churchyard; an unexpected sight amongst the sober gravestones.

Up on the hill...
Photo by Eileen Rennison.

...And Down in the Lockup.

Earlier generations without the benefits of the welfare state, no unemployment pay, widow's pensions or retirement pensions lived in fear of 'ending up in the workhouse'. Should they lose their jobs, be unable to work, or have no family able to support them in their old age, without money that was their only relief. The workhouses were usually bleak institutions where families and husbands and wives were separated; where all who were able-bodied were expected to perform manual and menial tasks as payment for their bare accommodation and food. Unemployed men tramping the country were given overnight accommodation on the same basis. This system of providing for the poor and destitute was still in place up to the 1940s, and many of the old buildings, now converted to other uses, still remain.

Workhouse Farm at Holme-upon Spalding Moor still retains a relic of those days in a narrow tower-like building said to have been the lockup of the one time workhouse there, into which any stroppy paupers were presumably thrust. Its high walls have only small slits near the top, making it a dark grim prospect; a cold and cruel punishment to modern thinking, whatever one's fault may have been.

Look out along the Howden road on the way to Workhouse Farm for a signpost directing one to Land of Nod! I did not follow the sign and do not know what kind of place it might be. A sleepy village perhaps? Or an ideal home for insomniacs? I expect this evocative name probably has a simple, even prosaic meaning - but I prefer not to know it!

...And down in the lock-up.

Photo by Richard Hebblethwaite.

21. HORNSEA

Hornsea is on the coast about 15 miles south of Bridlington and a similar distance north of Hull. It is 12 miles from Beverley on the A1035 and B1244. The Tower is in Willows Drive across from the Museum. St. Nicholas church is nearby. All are in the main street, Newbegin. The church is open in the summer and at other times on application to the vicarage.

A Singular Signal Tower.

In 1844 a Mr. W. Bettison built a circular tower which still stands in Hornsea. Fifty feet tall, with bricks laid in a decorative style and a crenellated top, it is an unusual building with an even more unusual purpose. I understand that it was intended as a lookout from which a servant kept watch for the approach of the master. On seeing his carriage in the distance he would then pass on the information to the kitchen staff in order that they could make ready his meal without delay. It seems Mr. Bettison must have been a stickler for punctuality and prompt service - or a man with a healthy appetite that couldn't wait!

Underground, Underhand.

Parish churches with a crypt beneath them are not common. St Nicholas' church in Hornsea has a crypt with two rooms one of which contains a fireplace. It is a crypt, if we are to believe the stories about it, with an unorthodox and somewhat disreputable past. It is said to have been at one time the home of a witch, Nanny Cankerneedle, though she may well have been simply a poor, eccentric but harmless old woman; such women have often in the past been accused of witchcraft. The church which now has a tower, originally had a spire, until the night in a storm when it came crashing down onto the church. A verger at that moment illicitly using the crypt as a store for smuggled goods, in his fear and guilt, took this to be divine retribution and suffered a stroke from which he never recovered. Today the crypt is restored to respectability, being used as a store for the more mundane church stone and ladders. The entry from inside the church is now blocked off and the outside door securely locked.

Should you leave Hornsea on the B1244, which runs alongside the Mere, the largest freshwater lake in Yorkshire, be sure to keep a lookout to the right for the delightful round cottage, which despite its unusual circular construction I am assured has normal rectangular rooms.

Right:
A singular tower. Photo by Richard Hebblethwaite.

Below:
Underground, underhand.

Photo by Eileen Rennison.

22. HUNMANBY

Straying Man, Straying Beast.

From Filey follow the A1039 about 1³/₄ miles to Muston. Turn left there for a further 1¹/₂ miles approximately to Hunmanby. From Malton take the A64 to the roundabout at Staxton (about 16 miles), then join the A1039 for 2¹/₂ miles. Turn right to Hunmanby, a further 2³/₄ miles.
The pound and lockup are on the village green.

At one time many villages had a pound, pen- or pinfold, different names for the enclosure in which straying animals could be penned or impounded, until such time as their owners reclaimed them, perhaps paying a small fee to the man in charge, known as the pinder; one of those many occupations which have given us present day surnames. In similar fashion some villages had a lock-up cell in which villagers who strayed from the path of sobriety or the law, could be held until they sobered up or could be handed over to a higher authority. Hunmanby is unusual in that it has both a pinfold and a lock-up, situated right next to each other on the village green. The lock-up has not one but two small cells, with narrow doors and tiny windows, offering less spacious accommodation, and seemingly no more comfort than the circular pinfold next door, but having at least the advantage of a roof!

Above:
Straying Man.

Below:
Straying Beast.

Photos by Richard Hebblethwaite.

23. KEYINGHAM

Keyingham is about 7 miles east of Hull on the A1033.

Two Mills.

The last complete windmill in Yorkshire can be seen at Skidby about 4 miles south of Beverley and $5\frac{1}{2}$ miles from Hull off the A164. Its black tarred tower with white cap and sails is a well-known landmark and its museum a popular attraction. The whole of East Yorkshire was once well provided with windmills, particularly the flatlands of Holderness, where like the Netherlands, they were a familiar sight. Now, no longer functional and in varying states of disuse and disrepair, they still remain a feature of the landscape. What other village however, even in the heyday of wind power could boast of two windmills, as Keyingham? The one to the west of the village was working up to World War II; the one on the eastern side lost its sails in a gale so fierce that pieces were found in the next village. Both today are delightfully converted to dwellings.

Two Mills.
Photos by Eileen Rennison.

24. KILHAM

Things Ancient and Modern.

From Bridlington take the A166 road to Driffield for about 6¼ miles, then turn right. Continue for another 1½ miles, then turn left to the village. The church stands ahead on a corner opposite the Star Inn.
From Beverley take the A164 for about 12¼ miles to the Driffield bypass, from there taking the A166 road to Bridlington for a further 4½ miles approximately before turning left. Continue about 1½ miles, then turn left into the village. The church will be seen ahead.

Right:
Needlework Kneelers.

Below:
The Bull Ring.

Once the most important market town on the Wolds, Kilham's title of 'Capital of the Wolds' was gradually taken over by Driffield towards the end of the 18th century. Though taking a pride in its history which goes back as far as the Ice Age, Kilham is today a thriving and modern community. A relic of the past can be seen in the small grass verge below the churchyard wall. An iron ring, embedded in a stone, to which a bull would have been tethered, is a reminder of the barbaric baiting of animals which was once enjoyed as entertainment by our ancestors. Inside the church can be seen a modern use of leisure time in the form of beautiful needlework kneelers presumably executed by parishioners and commemorating local people and events with unusual and original designs. These include such delightful motifs as a picture by Claude Monet, a farmer sowing seeds, and perhaps most unusual and unexpected in church, a red motor-car on a moorland road.

Outside in the churchyard is a sundial set on a strange old stone shaped like a small empty coffin. During World War II Kilham had the unusual and surprising privilege of being the station of the Pigeon Corps, which played an important, if little known part in communications, carrying messages by pigeon when secrecy was a factor or when other means of communication were not possible or had failed. A recent article in a local newspaper told a story of two pigeons posthumously decorated for some heroic efforts which resulted in lives saved, though whether they were stationed at Kilham it did not say.

Right:
Churchyard Sundial.

Photos by Eileen Rennison.

25. KILNSEA

Kilnsea is on the Spurn Penisula. From Hull take the A1033 for about 12$\frac{1}{2}$ miles, then the B1445 for about 6 miles, then continue through Easington to Kilnsea, a further 3 miles. Park by the Blue Bell Information Centre and follow the lane which goes alongside the caravan village opposite. The sound mirror is to the left across fields opposite the Beacon Lagoons Nature Reserve board.

A Concrete Sound Mirror.

It is not easy to get close to this extraordinary object, bearing in mind that it entails a walk of a quarter hour or more along a very rough track only to find the hazards of an electric fence and crops in the field where it stands. I would strongly recommend binoculars. It can be viewed across the fields to the left on approaching Kilnsea as well as from where the Beacon Lagoons Nature Reserve board is located. The huge device, reminding me of an enormous concrete satellite dish, is believed to have been used to locate enemy aircraft or Zeppelins by the reflected sound of their engines but little is known of when it was actually constructed. Approximately 4 metres high, 4$\frac{1}{2}$ metres wide and 2 metres deep at its base, it consists of a concave area in front of which stands a metal post to which a microphone was attached. One wonders how efficient it was as part of our coastal defences in this open and isolated strip of land and whether it has ever been tested out. An interesting plaque on the Blue Bell wall gives a startling indication of how this part of the coast is being eroded, stating as it does, that the house when built in 1847 stood 530 yds from the sea, but by 1994 when it was restored the distance was reduced to only 190 yds.

A concrete sound mirror.
Photo by K.T. Watson.

26. KINGSTON UPON HULL

Hull is approximately 40 miles east of York and 10 miles beyond Beverley on the A1079.

It is about 27 miles south of Bridlington on the A165. Ye Olde White Harte is in Silver Street.

Hull Transport Museum is in High Street next to Wilberforce House. It is open Monday to Saturday 10am -5pm. Sunday 1.30-4.30pm.

Skelton's Bakery is in Paragon Street.

The Plotting Parlour.

The streets of Hull (or to give it its full title of Kingston-upon-Hull) are rich in statuary and memorials. Where else can one see a huge golden equestrian statue dominating the passing traffic, a 90 feet high Doric column commemorating William Wilberforce (1759 - 1833) the great campaigner against slavery, or so many large and heroic carvings decorating the buildings. It is a city full of history, though not all the reminders of it are to be seen on the street. Tucked away down a passage in Silver Street Ye Olde White Harte Inn was once the scene of a unique and memorable event. In 1642 Sir John Hotham, a parliamentarian and Governor of Hull, together with the city's two MPs and other dignitaries, met in the parlour of Ye Olde White Harte, then his residence, to discuss the plan to hold the city against the King. On April 23rd 1642 the gates of the then walled city were duly closed against the King, and his entry refused. By June of

of that year the Civil War between Charles I and the Parliamentarians had begun. In 1645 both Sir John and his son were accused of changing their allegiance and communicating with the Royalists, and were beheaded. Today, one can sit in that dark panelled room, now known as the Plotting Parlour, with its old carved dresser, swords and pictures of Cavaliers hanging around it, and try to imagine the heart-searching discussion that must have taken place there, so long ago, before the far-reaching decision to defy the King was made.

Left:
The Plotting Parlour.

Below:
Strange Name -
Land of Green Ginger.

Photos by
Eileen Rennison.

Strange Names and a Literary Connection.

Hull has many unusually named little streets: Dagger Lane, Bowlalley Lane, Fish Street, Sewer Lane, the origins of which it is at least possible to guess. But if one takes two right turns on leaving Ye Old White Harte in Silver Street one comes to what must surely be the most romantic sounding and mysterious, the Land of Green Ginger. I have been told it derived its strange name from the fact that this was the area where imported ginger was brought ashore and sold. What is certain is that it provided Winifred Holtby, the author who grew up in Rudston not far away, and whose love of East Yorkshire inspired her books, with the title for one of her novels, published in 1927.

Transports of Strange Delight.

It is possible that in the latter half of the 19th century an unusual means of locomotion was to be seen in the streets of Hull, its rider busily propelling it with the use of both hands and feet. The four-wheeled velocipede with its heavy wooden frame, its iron wheels and system of pedals and levers and abdominal steering, was built by   W. Hodgson of Hull as an intended improvement on the two-wheeled 'boneshaker' type. It is still possible to see and marvel at this amazing contraption in the Hull Transport Museum in High Street, where one can compare it with other machines in the evolution of the cycle. The museum is full of interest, from the usual three-wheeled Hansom cab reputed to have been used by Edward VII, to the oldest tram in the country. Built in 1867 for a German Royal Visit to the Isle of Wight, the tram's richly carved body of teak and mahogany with its design of monograms and grapes gave it the name of Grape Car. When it was taken out of service in 1935 it was the oldest working tram in the country. With only about fourteen years separating them it is interesting to compare its elaborate and polished workmanship with the plain, almost rough appearance of the Quadricycle. But undoubtedly the strangest vehicle in the collection of the museum - though not presently on display - is to my mind, the colourful and exotic sleigh of Lady Chesterfield from Nunburnholme on the Wolds. This fabulous sleigh of Russian design, straight out of a fairy tale, must have presented a strange sight conveying her Ladyship around the Wolds villages. It is even said to have once been seen in Hull market. Gliding over the snow, drawn by a high-stepping pony, seated in her upholstered shell, a swan's neck and head rearing up from the carved runners and a unicorn in front pointing the way with his horn, she must have caused even the not-easily-impressed Yorshire folk to stop and stare.

Transport of strange delight.

A Unique Service.

There is one feature in Hull which is quite unique - its telephone system. The observant visitor will have noticed its distinctive white telephone boxes and perhaps wondered why they should be different from boxes in other towns. The reason is that Hull's telephone system was never part of the national service. In 1904 Hull City Council opened its first exchange, making it for many years the only municipal telephone company in the country, with calls costing as little as one old penny. Since privatisation of the national telephone system Hull remains unique, being now the only publicly-owned service in the country.

Old Mother Riley.

Arthur Lucan was born in 1887 and began his stage career a year after leaving school at the age of thirteen. He met his Irish wife Kitty McShane while on tour in Dublin and they married when she was only fifteen. Between the wars the husband and wife team in the guise of Old Mother Riley the Irish washerwoman and her daughter, amused audiences throughout the country with their antics on stage and screen. By the middle of the 1920s they were top of the bill in variety and in the early 1930s had played at the London Palladium and appeared at a Royal Variety Performance. The 1940s saw the film debut of Old Mother Riley and her daughter. Lucan, wearing black bonnet askew on a grey wig, boots, long skirt and apron and shawl, in constant confrontation with an errant daughter, gave hilarious emphasis to their comic rows and quarrels, with the pantomime contortions and gestures of his seemingly double-jointed limbs and mobile features.

He/she was perpetually blundering into situations which resulted in utter chaos from which he/she nevertheless invariably came out top. The relationship between the couple was always volatile off-stage as well as on, and by 1951 their marriage had fallen apart. Lucan attempted to carry on in variety alone but without great success. On May 17th 1954 waiting in the wings to go on stage in Hull he suffered a massive heart attack and died. His comic genius is not forgotten in Hull, but is commemorated in the unexpected setting of Skelton's Bakery in Paragon Street. There in an alcove at the rear of the cafeteria, a bust of Lucan in the role of Old Mother Riley was unveiled in 1986 by Danny La Rue, the well-known female impersonator. Framed by red velvet curtains like the proscenium of a theatre he makes his last theatrical appearance for his many friends and admirers in the city where his long and talented career came to an end.

A unique service.

Old mother Riley.

27. KIRBY GRINDALYTHE

Ascension Mosaic.

From Malton take the B1248 for about 5 miles to North Grimston. About 2 miles further, fork left to Duggleby then a further 1³/₄ miles to Kirby Grindalythe. Turn right into the village, then right again to the church.

From York take the A166 to Driffield for about 19 miles. Then just through Fridaythorpe turn left on the B1251 to Sledmere, approximately a further 9 miles. In Sledmere turn left beside the monuments to Kirby Grindalythe 2¹/₂ miles. Entering the village turn left for the church.

From Driffield take the B1252 to Sledmere about 8 miles. Go through the village and turn right beside the monuments a further 2¹/₂ miles to Kirby Grindalythe. Turn left to the church.

In the little village of Kirby Grindalythe St. Andrew's church is yet another of the 'Sykes' churches' of the Wolds, restored by Sir Tatton Sykes in the late 19th century. It contains a breath-taking mosaic of the Ascension, covering the entire wall of the tower arch. The work of Italian craftsmen, using tesserae as small as a fingernail, the detailed and colourful mosaic shows the figure of Christ above the arch, holding an open book with the words *Ego sum resurrectio et vita.* (I am the Resurrection and the Life). The Virgin Mary and the eleven Apostles are grouped on either side in attitudes of adoration. Aside from its religious message it is a magnificent work of art and craftsmanship, that fills one with admiration for the skill, the time and the patience which must have gone into the enormous task of producing it.

Ascension Mosaic.
Photo by Eileen Rennison.

28. LANGTOFT

Freak Weather Record.

From Bridlington take the B1253 road to Octon roundabout, about 10 miles. Turn left on the B1249 to Langtoft, a further 1½ miles.
From Driffield, Langtoft is about 6 miles north on the B1249. Back Street is off the main village road alongside the Ship Inn.

After a heavy snowstorm like many others on the Wolds, the village of Langtoft can, even today, be cut off from the outside world. In the past it has suffered what one might feel is more than its fair share of disaster from freak weather. In May 1853 two ploughmen narrowly escaped with their lives when their ploughs were destroyed and their horses killed by lightning in a terrible thunderstorm. In June 1888 a waterspout washed mud and boulders down from the hills into the village streets, sweeping small household articles along with it into the village pond.

The two most notorious 'Great Floods' of 1657 and 1892 are on permanent record in the village, showing the height to which the flood water rose. After the cloudburst in July 1892 the water rushed through the village and down Back Street, forcing its way into one house through a front window and out through the back door, taking with it the furniture, and the joiner's shop, tools and wood stock. A commemorative plaque can be seen in Back Street. Reading it on a sunny summer's day in this pleasant village, one can imagine the shock and devastation the unexpected violent weather caused here so often in the past at this time of year, and thank heaven for modern day drainage systems!

Freak weather record.

Photo by Eileen Rennison.

29. LANGTON

The Perfect Wife.

Take the B1248 from Malton for about 6 miles to North Grimston. Turn right just before reaching the village, to Langton, about a further 2 1/2 miles. The church is on the left at the far end of the village, behind some very large trees.

From Beverley take the A164 out to join the B1248. Follow the signs for Malton as far as North Grimston about 22 miles. Take a left turn just beyond the village to Langton, about 2 1/2 miles.

Mary Ingram, the wife of Thomas Ingram of Temple Newsam, near Leeds, died in 1656 giving birth to twins. She was the sister-in-law of Lady Norcliffe of Langton, and her painted effigy with two small babies, guarded by angels, can be seen in the Chancel of the church there.

The facts are recorded on her tomb and her virtues are lauded by her grieving husband in the following words -

'Readers with reverence approach this tombe,
Here lyes A Pattern for the times to come,
The glorious envy of her sex where all
Virtues and glories were habituall;
A wife as one would wish; be this her pride,
She nere displeased her husband till she dyde.'

What wife could ever hope for a better, more glowing reference? Alas, too late for Mary to see! We can only hope for her sake that her husband

The perfect wife.

Photo by Eileen Rennison.

30. LOWTHORPE

Family Tree.

On the A166 road from Driffield to Bridlington take a right turn after about 3¹/₂ miles. Continue for a further ³/₄ mile. The church is on the left down a path lined with evergreens. From Bridlington on the A166 take a left turn after about 8 miles, then continue as above.

St. Martin's church is situated on the edge of a wood at the outskirts of the village of Lowthorpe, at the end of a long pathway lined with closely-planted tall dark evergreens. Its Romantic atmosphere is heightened by the fact that the chancel is a roofless ruin, blocked off from the nave, which with the tower now constitutes the entire church. In the 1800s it seems that there were trees actually growing within the chancel, which must have presented a very strange sight - but no stranger sight than a tree which may still be seen inside the church on a most unusual monument. No one is sure whose monument it is, but it is thought to be that of Sir Thomas Heslerton who died in the late 14th century. Two figures, male and female, lie under a sheet, over which a tree spreads its roots to their feet and its branches sideways across their bodies. At the end of each branch is a small head, seven on the man's side and six on the woman's. These may possibly represent their children, forming a weird and unusual 'family tree'.

On the wall nearby is another interesting item; a stone bearing the final message of a world-weary man.

'Farewell vain world, I've had enough of thee,
And now am careless what thou sayest of me.
Thy smiles I court not nor thy frowns I fear,
My cares are past. My head lies quiet here.'
It fills one with curiosity to know more about him and raises many intriguing questions!

Family tree.
Photo by Richard Hebblethwaite.

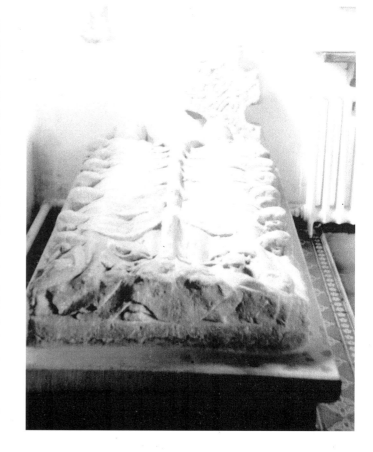

31. LUND

American Connection, a Gateway and Guns.

Take the B1248 road from Beverley to Malton for about 6 miles then take a right turn into Lund. In the village turn left to the green. The gateway is next to the church.

Or from Pocklington on the B1246 to Driffield through Warter and North Dalton - about 9 miles. Take a right turn at the beginning of the village to and through Middleton-on-the-Wolds approximately 3 miles to the B1248. Turn right for about ¼ mile then left into the village.

The little village of Lund between Beverley and Driffield is centred around a green, on which stands an ancient market cross that has lost its top and leans slightly from repeated repairs over the centuries.

Beside the green, next to the old forge now converted to a bus shelter, is the church and beyond that behind a wall with a beautiful gateway is the manor house, built in the 18th century on the site of an earlier house. The gateway was erected in the 17th century by the lords of the manor, the Remington family. Records show the family to have been connected with this area from the 16th to the 18th century when they emigrated to America. There they founded the famous company, internationally known for the rifle, small arms and typewriter of that name, thus forging an unexpected link between this quiet rural corner of East Yorkshire and the commercial world of the United States.

Left:
The market cross.

Right:
Gateway to the manor.

Photos by
Eileen Rennison.

32. LYTHE

Ophicleides and Wrestlers.

Lythe is about 4 miles north of Whitby on the A174. Follow the signposting to Sandsend, and through it, up the steep Lythe Bank. The church is on the right just before the village is reached. Parking is possible in a lane on the right immediately past the church.

When I heard that St. Oswald's Church at Lythe contained two ophicleides I had to turn to my dictionary to discover what I might find there. Others, more knowledgeable, will know that an ophicleide is a rare and obsolete musical instrument; a long trumpet-ended tube turned back on itself. I found the large black wind instruments hanging on the wall each side of a door, reaching more than half-way down its height. They were once used in the Church to support the singing in the Choir but it is hard to imagine anyone playing such heavy and clumsy-looking instruments or indeed what kind of sound they might make.

An interesting carved stone in the same area of the Church, shows what seems to be figures engaged in a wrestling bout. This is one of several old fragments of stone found built into the walls of the old Church at its restoration in 1910. They are of Anglo-Danish design and come from a Danish graveyard which owed its origin to the settlers following the Viking landing near Lythe in 867.

The Church standing high on the hill can be seen from miles around, from both land and sea. The name of Lythe means 'on the hill' and the view as one travels back down Lythe Bank to Sandsend and Whitby is quite spectacular. Almost worth a visit for itself alone!

Ophicleides.
Photo by Eileen Rennison.

33. MARKET WEIGHTON

The Yorkshire Giant.

On the A1079 road from York to Beverley, about 18½ miles from York turn left off the Market Weighton by pass into the town.
From Beverley take the A1035 for about 2 miles to join the A1079, then continue for a further 7½ miles.
From Hull on the A1079 after about 17½ miles turn right off the bypass into the town .
Bradley house is on York Road.

William Bradley was born in Market Weighton in February 1787 and died of consumption aged thirty-three in 1820; a short life but not very unusual for the times. On his death he was secretly buried, and many years later reburied inside All Saints church as a precaution against bodysnatchers. His body would have made a fine and unusual prize for them.
One of thirteen siblings of normal size, he grew from his birth weight of 14 lbs to a height of 7 ft 9 ins, weighed 27 stones and was well proportioned in build. As the 'tallest man ever recorded in England' he made himself a good living exhibiting himself at fairgrounds and shows. Who knows? - today he might possibly have become a basket ball player!

A plaque depicting his fifteen inches long and five and a half inches wide footprint marks the house - now a cycle shop - where he lived, situated at the junction of two roads on York road, opposite the Bay Horse. On a wall inside the shop is a life-size painting executed by a local art teacher from.an

etching of the Yorkshire giant - and beside my 5ft 2ins he seemed a giant indeed!

It is interesting that Shiptonthorpe, the next village, was the birthplace of one, Edwin Calvert, who never grew beyond 36 ins and drank himself to death at the age of seventeen, in contrast to Bradley who was abstemious and moderate in all things.

The Yorkshire Giant.

*Photos by
Eileen Rennison.*

34. MELBOURNE

A Corrugated Church.

From York take the A1079 road to Hull for about 3¹/₂ miles to Grimston roundabout then take the B1228 to the right through Elvington and Sutton upon Derwent, leavng the B1228 after about 7¹/₂ miles to go straight ahead to Melbourne a further 1¹/₂ miles.

The church is at the end of St. Monica's Close, off to the right almost opposite the Cross Keys Inn.

From Pocklington take the B1247 for about 1¹/₂ miles to join the A1079, then turn right for 1¹/₄ miles and left to Allerthorpe, and on a further 4 miles to Melbourne. Turn left into St. Monica's Close.

Towards the end of the 19th century a temporary church made of corrugated iron was erected in the village of Melbourne. It was intended, eventually, to replace it with a stone building, but for whatever reason that was never achieved, and so more than a hundred years later the corrugated church still remains to serve the village.

If the thought of corrugated iron suggests something of a basic and shed-like appearance nothing could be further from the truth with regard to the pretty little church at Melbourne, with its grey painted walls, red roof and steeple, and flower-edged path leading up to the door. I have heard it described as a 'Tin Tabernacle'; a somewhat mocking and derogatory name for a charming and most unusual church, but perhaps it is just an affectionate nickname for a church which I feel must surely inspire affection. The church, which is a grade-two listed building, was not open when I visited, and so I was not able to go inside, but peeping through a window it looked as pleasant inside as it is out. I couldn't help wondering though whether the pattering of rain on the roof in bad weather might distract one from the service.

A corrugated church.
Photo by Eileen Rennison.

35. MILLINGTON

Gaits and The Gate.

From Pocklington take the road signposted to Millington for about 2¹/₂ miles, then a right turn down into the village. The inn is on the main village street.
From Driffield take the A163 for about 5 miles to a roundabout. From there take the B1246 for about 11 miles, through North Dalton and Warter to Pocklington. Then as above.

Millington is thought to have been the Roman Delgovicia, a settlement established there on the Roman route from the coast because of the presence of the waters of Millington springs. Certainly half a mile from the village the foundations of a circular temple and other buildings were discovered as well as Roman pavements, coins and tiles.
Today Millington is on the Wolds Way; an attraction for walkers and popular with families enjoying outings and picnics at nearby Millington Wood and Millington Pastures. The wood is an ancient ash wood and a Site of Special Scientific Interest. The Pastures were awarded to the parish by an Act of Parliament in 1770 at the time of the Enclosures. They were divided or 'stinted' out to the local farmers in 'gaits', the name given to pasturage for a specified number of sheep; the number of 'gaits' awarded to each farmer being proportional to the land he had in the parish before enclosure.
In the main street the village inn bears the unusual name of The Gate: this must surely be a corruption of the word 'gait' and derive from the grazing rights on the Pastures. As well as its unusual name an interesting feature inside the pub is a ceiling depicting a map of the area.

At the end of the street, by Town Farm, an iron ring in the pavement may be a puzzle to all but the oldest generation, who will recognise it as a hooping iron used in the shaping of cartwheels, in the days when the job of the blacksmith and wheelwright was an important one in a farming community.

Left:
The hooping iron.

Photo by
Eileen Rennison.

Below:
Gaits and the Gate.

Photo by
Richard Hebblethwaite.

36. NORTH GRIMSTON

The Lord's Supper on a Font.

North Grimston is on the B1248 Malton to Beverley road 6 miles from Malton. The church is on the left just before entering the village. From Beverley take the A164 to Driffield for about 1 mile, then take the B1248 to the left and follow the signs to Malton about 22 miles. Continue through the village and the church is on the right as one leaves.

The church of St. Nicholas at North Grimston is very old; plain and simple without and within. But within that plain interior stands a wonderful treasure which is probably older than the church itself. Far from plain, the font is said by some to be Norman like parts of the church. The entire surface of its straight sided, heavy tub-like shape is covered with crude but clear carvings, suggestive of an even earlier period. One half of the surface shows the Lord and his Disciples at the Last Supper, with details of the meal - fish, bread and goblets - all clearly depicted on the table. The other half shows the Descent from the Cross, and St. Nicholas.

The church also has the unique feature of two internal buttresses. At the rear of the Nave I was somewhat surprised to see an old-fashioned plough painted a very bright blue making a splash of colour against the wall.

There are other curious, primitively carved fonts to be seen in this area, at Langtoft and Kirkburn near Driffield, and Cowlam near Sledmere.

The Lord's Supper on a font.
Photo by Richard Hebblethwaite.

Sixty-five Thousand Shoes.

Passing through North Grimston village one may see, just within a gateway, some curious rusty-brown coloured erections with a textured surface, and crescent shape decorating the top. Are they pieces of modern sculpture, one might wonder, or relics of the past? They could perhaps be regarded as both! On closer inspection they prove to be built entirely from rusty discarded horseshoes. There are an estimated sixty-five thousand old shoes in the two columns at the entrance, and further back, twenty-five and a half thousand on an incomplete column which is still being added to because this is a working forge.

They were built, I was told, for the practical purpose

50

of tidiness, but it could be argued that they have as much or even more artistic merit than the notorious bricks in the Tate Gallery in London. Be that as it may, they are an unusual and tangible testimony to the past and present work of the farrier in this area, where horses, though no longer used for heavy work on the farm, are still an important feature.

Sixty-five thousand shoes.
Photo by Richard Hebblethwaite.

37. POCKLINGTON

The Flying Man.

Pocklington is approximately $15\frac{1}{2}$ miles from Driffield and about $13\frac{1}{4}$ miles from York. From Driffield take the A163 road for about 5 miles, then the B1246 a further $10\frac{1}{2}$ miles to Pocklington.

From York take the A1079 turning left to Barmby Moor after about $11\frac{1}{2}$ miles. Pocklington is then about $1\frac{3}{4}$ miles.

The church is in a central position near the market.

Flying men were a familiar sight in Pocklington during the Second World War. They flew on dangerous missions from the airfields that surrounded the town in machines which were the best of their time. Their purpose was the serious one of war and inevitably there were tragic deaths.

Two centuries earlier a very different flying man was to be seen in Pocklington. Travelling around the country from his home in Lincolnshire his purpose was to amuse and entertain people with a daring display of flying. Thomas Pelling flew with batlike fabric wings attached to his arms and legs, one ankle attached to a pulley on a rope stretched from a suitable high point - in Pocklington the church tower - to a windlass on the ground some distance away. On 10th April 1733, as an expectant crowd watched, something went wrong with his dangerous act. The rope slackened and Pelling was dashed to his death against the church. A memorial on the outside wall of the chancel commemorates the exploit and Thomas Pelling's untimely and unusual death.

Europe's Largest Collection of Water-Lilies.

The visitor to Pocklington in the months of June or July will find the water-lilies in Burnby Hall Gardens a spectacular sight, and having seen them will not be surprised to learn that they are Europe's largest collection of these beautiful flowers and officially recognised as the national collection in Britain; an unexpected but well-deserved distinction to find in a Yorkshire market town.

The small museum in the gardens also merits a visit from the seeker after the unusual, being full of many strange and exotic items collected by the late Major Percy Stewart. The gardens are well signposted from the centre of the town.

Above:
The flying man.

Left:
Europe's largest collection
of water lilies.

Photos by Richard Hebblethwaite.

38. REDCAR

Redcar is on the coast north of Whitby. Take the A174 for about 23 miles, through Saltburn, then join the A1085 for a further 5 miles approximately to Redcar.

The Zetland Museum is on the Esplanade at the corner with King Street and next to the Royal Hotel. It is open May to September daily from 11.00 to 4.00. There is pay-and-display parking next to it.

The Oldest Lifeboat in the World.

Up until the end of the 18th century lifesaving was under-taken by local seamen in their boats, and even after the invention of boats specially designed for the task it remained purely a local operation. In 1789 the brig *Adventure was* wrecked at the mouth of the Tyne while people on shore watched helplessly as the crew drowned, because fishermen were unable to launch their boats in the huge seas. As a result of this tragedy a committee of business men was formed and two guineas offered for the design of a boat capable of mastering heavy seas and gales. Two of the designs submitted were considered practical, those of William Wouldhave and Henry Greathead. Wouldhave was offended by the offer of one guinea as a 'second prize' and stormed off leaving his design model behind. The committee then commissioned boatbuilder Greathead to build a lifeboat on a modified version of Woudhave's design. A copy of this boat stands on display in their home town of South Shields. Greathead went on to build thirty-one lifeboats of which only one, the *Zetland,* remains. Built in 1800 at a cost of £200 and brought to Redcar in 1802, it served for 78 years and saved 500 lives. It can still be seen in Redcar in the fascinating and informative little Zetland Museum housed in the old Boathouse on the Esplanade. As well as the *Zetland,* which in 1963 made the journey up to Edinburgh to be part of the World Exhibition of Lifeboats, the museum contains models of boats and ships, equipment and old photographs and upstairs a re-creation of a fisherman's cottage. The Laurie Picknett Gallery in the museum is named after a member of a local family with a long history of lifesaving. Thomas Hood Picknett, the last surviving crew member of the Zetland, died in 1935 at the age of eighty-nine.

The museum, like the Royal National Lifeboat Institute itself, is solely dependent on voluntary contributions and is a tribute to all connected with it. The Zetland lifeboat is a unique piece of seafaring history and a source of pride to Redcar.

The oldest lifeboat in the world.
Photo by Eileen Rennison.

39. ROBIN HOOD'S BAY

Exits for the Living and the Dead.

Robin Hood's Bay is on the coast about 5 miles south of Whitby and 12 miles north of Scarborough. From Whitby take the A171 for about 3 miles, then turn left onto the B1447 for about another 2½ miles.

There is parking on the edge of the village at the top of the cliff. The village consists of steep roads and many steps which may present problems for the old or unfit.

'Bay Town' as it is known to its inhabitants, is a steep and picturesque tumble of red-roofed houses down to the sea. In its narrow cobbled streets, alleys and courtyards, it is easy to imagine it, as it once was, a hotbed of smuggling, with the whole village engaged in the task of outwitting the Customs men. It is said that many of the old cottages have secret rooms and cupboards, even secret tunnels from house to house, to enable men to escape and goods to be hidden. One alley serving perhaps as an escape route not only from the Customs and Excise men, but also from that other one time scourge of seafarers, the press-gang, reminds us of the past with its name The Bolts. A particular feature of the houses, with an unusual purpose, and still to be seen today, are the 'coffin windows', so called because the staircases were so narrow and twisting that windows were needed on landings specifically to enable coffins, unable to negotiate the bends, to be lowered from them to the street. The best known

example, Littlewood Cottage, can be seen by turning left from the Dock up Tyson's Steps then left again after Sunnyside, but the visitor may like to see if others can be spotted. The late, once popular author, Leo Walmsley's books *Three Fevers* (which was later turned into a film) *Sally Lunn* and *Phantom Lobster,* were all centred on Robin Hood's Bay under the name of Bramblewick, and the surrounding area, which he knew and loved. Reprinted, his trilogy can be bought in shops in the village, and a blue plaque marks the house where he lived in the street heading down to the Dock.

The Bolts and Coffin window.
Photos by Eileen Rennison.

40. RUDSTON

The Devil's Javelin.

Rudston is about 4¹/₄ miles from Bridlington on the B1253. The church is on a high rise to the left of the road on entering the village. There is parking at the opposite side of the road.

The devil in a rage at the building of a church on a sacred pagan site hurled a gigantic stone javelin, in an attempt to destroy it, but fortunately missed. So says the popular legend, to explain the huge gritstone monolith which stands a mere twelve feet or so from the north-east corner of All Saints church at Rudston. It measures over 16 feet in circumference at its base and is almost 26 feet high. How it actually came to be there is a matter of uncertainty. The nearest source of gritstone is 10 miles away at Cayton Bay, representing a formidable feat of human effort to transport and erect such a huge stone, some 4000 years ago. The largest standing stone in the country, it almost certainly marked a pagan holy place which was taken over by the early Christians, as was often their practice, and - perhaps with a cross on the top - was assimilated into the new religion. It is a strange and awesome object to find amongst the gravestones. Rudston was the birthplace of Winifred Holtby, the Yorkshire author, who died tragically young at the age of thirty-seven. Her gravestone in the form of an open book can be seen in the churchyard. Also, nearby, a touching effigy of a young boy in short-trousered school uniform.

It is also interesting to know that the village sportsfield is rented from the local landowner for the unusual annual rent of one white rose.

The Devil's javelin.
Photo by Eileen Rennison.

41. SALTBURN

Saltburn is about 20 miles north of Whitby on the A174. Enter the Valley Gardens by the steps opposite Dundas Street East, just before reaching the Spa Hotel. Turn right and keep to the top path parallel to the road. The memorial can be found at a slightly lower level branching left.

Dual Role Portico.

Like so many sea-side resorts Saltburn grew up around the railway and owes its origin to the vision of Henry Pease, a Quaker and director of the Stockton and Darlington Railway. The charm of a typical Victorian resort is still evident today, with its cliff-lift down to the pier, its gardens and wooded walks. Within the Valley Gardens among the trees that line the paths, is the town's unusual Albert Memorial, once the classical portico of the railway station at Barnard Castle. It stands above a flight of rather worn and crumbling steps, though the portico itself appeared to have been recently refurbished when I visited. Its columns and pediment stand out against the surrounding greenery of the trees to make a surprising memorial not only to Prince Albert, but also to Henry Pease, whose gift it was to the town. An example perhaps of Victorian thrift and the spirit of 'waste not, want not'?

Dual role portico.

*Photo by
Eileen Rennison.*

42. SCARBOROUGH

Scarborough is on the coast about 17 miles north of Bridlington on the A165 or approximately 42 miles from York on the A64(T). The Rotunda Museum is on the South Bay at the southern end of the Foreshore where it joins Valley Road.

The Three Mariners Inn is at the opposite end of the Foreshore looking out over the Old Harbour.
St. Mary's Church and Anne Bronte's grave can be reached up steep lanes and steps from behind the Three Mariners Inn or through the town via Eastborough, Queen Street and Castle Road.

Study on Wheels.

Scarborough is England's oldest holiday resort; a spa since 1626, with the discovery by Anne Farrow of its medicinal water, and later gaining popularity as the first place to encourage sea-bathing for its health giving properties. Over the years it has gained many interesting and distinguished buildings. The Rotunda Museum with its unusual circular plan is one of them. It was built in 1829 by Scarborough Philosophical Society, to display the collection of fossils and geological rocks of William Smith (1769 - 1839), a native of Scarborough who was the first to identify the age of rocks by means of the fossils in the different strata, thus earning for himself the title of the Father of Geology. The layout of the museum, to Smith's own design, was originally in layers from floor to ceiling, showing the different periods in an unusual but easy to understand fashion. In order that they might better be seen he also installed a unique viewing platform on wheels, from which they could be studied as it was moved around the museum. Today the museum is largely given over to archaeological displays but the platform - though no longer working - is still there to be seen and the building itself remains as a commemoration of William Smith.

Study on wheels - The Rotunda Museum.
Photo by Eileen Rennison.

Smugglers' Inn.

The Three Mariners could easily be missed, tucked away as it is down a little alleyway between two of the more usual bright and colourful facades of typical seaside attractions overlooking the harbour. A plaque on the rear of the building with its Georgian doorway and green shutters, simply claims it to be 'one of the earliest public houses in the town'. It is no longer an inn, but a small maritime

Museum. The almost hidden entry at the front, through the alleyway and under what appears to be an old ship's figure-head over the door, gives it a fitting atmosphere for its past connections with smuggling, which is heightened by the secret cupboards and passages inside. More unusually the old inn, with its proximity to the harbour, was used at one time as a mortuary for the bodies of sailors brought ashore after disaster at sea. Such sad events are an inevitable part of the history of seafaring, but it is the romantic aspect of smuggling which gives the Three Mariners its appeal.

Anne Bronte's Grave.

The Parish Church of St. Mary and the churchyard where Anne Bronte lies buried, are high upon Castle Hill. The approach is possible through the town or by the steep Church Steps from the harbour area. Should one be fit enough to tackle the latter route, there is something satisfying about arriving at the top to pay tribute to the author's memory, having paused at intervals to enjoy the views over roof-tops and out over the sea, which she too must have enjoyed. Anne was the youngest of the famous Bronte sisters and though perhaps not the most talented of the three she was the author of *Agnes Grey* and *The Tenant of Wildfell Hall.* She had a great love and happy memories of Scarborough and came with her sister Charlotte on her last visit in 1849, desperately ill with consumption, in the hope that the sea air might do her good. Sadly she had no time to enjoy or benefit from her visit; she died within days of arriving. Her grave, well tended and with flowers growing on it, is in that part of the graveyard which lies beyond the lane alongside the church. She was just twenty-eight.

St. Mary's Church is an interesting and historic building. It was struck by cannon-fire in 1644 when Scarborough Castle was held by Sir Hugh Cholmley for the King and besieged by the Roundheads in the Civil War. In World War 2 the East window was destroyed and replaced in 1958 by the York stained glass artist Harry Stammers. The visitor should not fail to see his interesting depiction of animals and birds, many of them such as penguin, ostrich, butterfly, camel and mouse, unusual and unexpected in a church.

The Smugglers Inn. Anne Bronte's grave.

Photos by Eileen Rennison.

43. SEATON ROSS

Marking the Sunny Hours.

From York follow the instructions given for Melbourne then turn right towards the end of the village. Turn left after about ³/₄ mile (Dial House Farm is on the left about 1¹/₄ miles from this turn), continue about 1¹/₂ miles turning right into the village.

From Pocklington follow the previous instructions for Melbourne, then as above.

The traveller to Seaton Ross following the route that I have suggested cannot miss and yet may be surprised by the sight of the huge sundial on Dial Hall Farm. It spreads across the centre of the upper storey with its lowest point just above the front door. It was the work of the farmer William Watson, who lived from 1784 to 1857, but his interest and skill in the construction of sundials did not end there. In the main village street is yet another example - a dial twelve feet in diameter on the wall of a small cottage, encircling an upper window and reaching down to the window below. A third, though smaller dial, with an inscription, on the brick-built church is dated 1823.

All three make a lasting and unusual record of one man's interest and enthusiasm.

A Rebuke from the Grave.

As you walk up the path to the church at Seaton Ross, look out to the left for the gravestone of Margaret Harper who died in 1853. Margaret I believe was supposed by some to be a witch, though I do not know on what grounds. Certainly it seems she had her critics, but managed to have the last word in a cutting and telling message from the grave. Carved on her headstone are the words

> 'The faults you've seen in me strive to avoid
> Search your own hearts and you'll be well employed.'

It seems a shame that today such words would not be possible on a gravestone. The wonderful richness of graveyards of the past, which makes their study such a fascinating and rewarding thing, seems to have given way to a bland uniformity, with rules and regulations imposed on what may and may not be inscribed on a stone. Even the stones themselves lack variety, as may be seen in any modern cemetery Our ancestors will find us a dull lot, I fear.

Marking the sunny hours.

Photos by Eileen Rennison.
and by
Richard Hebblethwaite.

44. SETTRINGTON

Uncommon Birds.

Settrington is about 4 miles from Malton, through Norton, taking the B1248 road to Driffield, then a left turn off to Settrington, left again, then right into the village. Take a right turn in the village signposted to North Grimston then left to Settrington House.

Settrington village consists of mellow stone cottages, farms and houses, and the fine 18th century building, Settrington House. Most large country houses have imposing gateways, often adorned with coats of arms or birds or beast. Lions, griffins, eagles, horses, even dogs are commonplace; but surely not storks? The attractive wrought-iron gates at Settrington House not only incorporate these slender, unexpected birds, but they appear to be carrying in their claws the little bundles that the stork traditionally brings! It is possible that they are in fact scallop shells which I believe are the symbol of a pilgrim, though the former interpretation is more fun and more intriguing. They make an unusual and elegant motif in black and gilt, whatever they are truly carrying.

In the 19th century, like so many quiet country places of the time, Settrington could boast of a learned scholar as its rector. Isaac Taylor, who served there from 1875 until his death in 1901, was known as the Darwin of Philology, for his study of names and alphabets. His memorial can be seen in the church.

Uncommon birds.

Photo by Eileen Rennison.

45. SLEDMERE

The Waggoners' Memorial.

Sledmere is 17 miles from Bridlington on the B1253. The monuments are through the village, past Sledmere House, on the right.
From Driffield Sledmere is 8 miles on the B1252.
From Malton take the B1248 road to Beverley through Norton. Turn left after about 5 miles just beyond North Grimston, to Duggleby and Sledmere, a further 6 miles.
From York take the A166 to Driffield and Bridlington about 19 miles to Fridaythorpe, then turn left on the B1251 to Sledmere, approx. a further 9 miles.
From York or Malton the memorials are on the left on the out-skirts of the village. There is parking space close by. The House is open to the public from April 30 to October 1, except Monday and Friday.

When Lancelot 'Capability' Brown landscaped the grounds of Sledmere House in the 1770s, the entire village of Sledmere was demolished to achieve his plan, and rebuilt in its present location. The Sykes family, who still live in the beautiful house, have over the centuries left their mark in the way of buildings and improvements on the entire Wolds.

As well as many interesting features in the house and grounds there are monuments in the village of an elaborate and curious nature. Opposite the entrance to the house is the domed memorial to Sir Christopher Sykes who died in 1801. Sir Tatton Sykes built his own memorial on the edge of the village in 1895, a copy of an Eleanor Cross (so called after the crosses erected by King Edward I at the places where his queen Eleanor's body rested on its journey from Nottinghamshire to burial at Westminster). This was later converted into the Village War Memorial.

But perhaps the most fascinating and unusual is the Waggoners' Memorial. In 1912 Lt. Colonel Sir Mark Sykes, the 6th Baronet, raised the Waggoners Reserve of farm workers skilled with horses, from the Wolds around Sledmere. In 1914 they were called up and provided transport for the British Expeditionary Force in France. Their service in the war was commemorated by Sir Mark with this memorial of his own design. Around the squat solid column at the centre of it, carvings in imitation of the Saxon style depict the story of the Waggoners, leaving their families and fields, crossing the sea and on the battle fields. The German soldiers are portrayed in the carvings as vicious caricatures, involved in brutal atrocities, in marked contrast to their calm English opponents; a reflection of anti-German feeling at the time, depicted in a way which would be unthinkable today. The last survivor of the Waggoners Reserve died in 1993.

The Waggoners' memorial.
Photo by Eileen Rennison.

46. SLEIGHTS

The First Hit.

Sleights is about 17 miles from Pickering on the A169 road to Whitby. From Whitby it is about 5 miles, turning left after about 2 miles from the A171 Whitby to Guisborough road on to the A169. The plaque is at this road junction.

Where the road from Sleights meets the road from Whitby to Guisborough a squat stone pillar with a plaque marks the spot where the first enemy aircraft to be shot down in World War Two crashed into a row of sycamores. It was the 3rd February 1940 when the Heinkel bomber was met and engaged two miles off the coast by a Hurricane fighter from RAF Acklington. The pilot, Group Captain Peter Townsend who was later to become well known for his romance with Princess Margaret, pursued the crippled plane inland, its rear gunner despite severe wounds returning his fire all the way. Peter Townsend, in respect for a brave enemy later visited Karl Missy in Whitby hospital, where one of his legs had to be amputated, and met up with him once again much later in Germany after the war. A friendly gesture, which to this writer at least symbolises the futility of war!

Between Sleights and the road junction where the plaque is, look out to the left for a sign for Featherbed Lane, often described as the narrowest highway in England. This mysteriously named stone-paved way is only about 3 or 4 feet wide, an

old stone 'trod' intended as a dry route for pack-ponies carrying goods between villages.

The first hit.
Photo by Eileen Rennison.

47. STAMFORD BRIDGE

The Battle of 1066.

Stamford Bridge lies about 8 miles from York on the A166 road to Bridlington. The commemorative stone is near the old mill, on the main street of the village.

On the 25th September 1066 Harold, King of England fought, defeated and killed Harald Hardrada the Norwegian, who, at the instigation of Harold's brother Tostig had invaded England, sailing up the Ouse to land at Riccall near York. Harold who was collecting his army in the south in expectation of a Norman invasion was obliged to march north to meet this threat. He offered generous terms to Tostig (and to Harald who was very tall, seven feet of English soil for his grave!), but to no avail. A fierce battle took place at the village of Stamford Bridge lasting almost an entire day and seeming at times as if the victory would go not to Harold but to the invaders. The battle over and won, Harold marched his men 260 miles back south to face the army of William of Normandy at the battle of Hastings on October 14th. Small wonder that Harold's army, which must surely have been exhausted was defeated there!

Today Stamford Bridge is a popular venue, its only invaders visitors, there to enjoy the pleasures of the riverside. They may also read and ponder the historic facts of that ancient battle, on a plaque on a rough weathered stone toward the end of the village. It stands on a patch of green close to the old watermill, near the site where the brothers' dispute led to the fierce battle that raged in the village.

The Battle of 1066.
Photo by Eileen Rennison.

48. SWINE

Swine is off the A165 between Hull and Skirlaugh. About 2 miles from Hull turn left at Coniston then a further 2¹/₂ miles. The Post Office and old blacksmith's shop are both on the right of the village street leading to the church.

Village Symbolism.

Swine is a small village away from the main roads and off the beaten tracks, but should you for any reason find yourself there or thereabouts, look out for the pretty little cottage which is the Post Office, its doorway surrounded by flowers and its amusing and charming sign announcing wordlessly the village name. The old doorway of the blacksmith's shop, now used for more modern business, is bricked up but its horseshoe shape, still clearly visible, tells of the work once carried out there.

Village symbolism.
Photos by Eileen Rennison.

49. UPLEATHAM

From Whitby take the A174 for about 16 miles to Brotton, turn left there onto the A173 for about 6 miles, then turn right onto the B1266 for a further 2 ¹/₂ miles to the church.

The Smallest Church in the Country.

St. Andrew's church, half a mile from the village of Upleatham, claims to be the smallest church in the country. Other churches in other parts of the country may lay claim to the same distinction but with its measurements of only 18 feet long and 15 feet wide the ancient church at Upleatham must surely have a strong case. Its suggestion of great age and traces of Norman architecture, its tiny tower and isolated situation, added to the universal appeal of the diminutive, make the church an interesting and unusual one.

The smallest church in the country.
Photo by Eileen Rennison.

50. WARTER

The Oldest Horse Race in England.

From Pocklington take the B1246 to Driffield for about 4¹/₂ miles to Warter and take a right turn in the village signposted to Market Weighton. After about 1¹/₂ miles at a T- junction turn left for a further ¹/₄ mile, then turn right. The post is on the left at the roadside about 1 mile on.

Or from Driffield on the A163 to York after about 11 miles, take a right turn signposted to Warter. The post is on the right grass verge about 100 yards on.

To the racing fraternity of high society March may be the month of the Cheltenham Gold Cup, but to the people of the East Yorkshire Wolds March means the Kiplingcotes Derby, reputed to be the oldest horse race in England, some would have it in the world! It has been run, on the third Thursday in March, over the same course, since it began. Even in the terrible winter of 1947, so I am reliably told, in the deep snow a horse was walked over the course simply so that the tradition should not be broken. The race, it is claimed, goes back as far as the 15th century but the accepted date as shown on the finishing post on a roadside not far from Warter, is 1519. The race begins at noon and is unique in that the weighing-in takes place at the winning post. Riders, who may be of either sex, must weigh at least 10 stone and any extra weight needed must be carried on the person not on the saddle. This rule, I am told, has led over the years to many layers of clothing being worn and some unusual objects being carried in pockets. It must also, I feel sure, have made for some uncomfortable rides! After the weighing-in the horses must then proceed to the starting point, an old stone post on a grass verge 4¹/₂ miles away towards Etton. The course runs across grass, along lanes, over a railway bridge and hard road.

Lord Burlington and a group of gentlemen originally endowed the race to the sum of £365, the winner to get the interest from it and the runner-up the entry fees. The interest being small on such a sum eventually led to the rider coming in second being better rewarded than the winner, and so in recent years a fixed first prize has been instituted to remedy this anomaly.

The village of Kiplingcotes has long since disappeared leaving nothing to show, but the race that bears its name goes on.

The Kiplingcotes Derby. Photos by Eileen Rennison.

51. WEAVERTHORPE

An Unusual Church and a Strange Object.

From Malton take the A64 road to Scarborough for about 11½ miles to Sherburn. Turn right at the crossroads in the village to Weaverthorpe, about a further 3¾ miles. The church is on the left before entering the village.

From Scarborough Sherburn is about 10½ miles on the A64. Take the left turn in the village, then as above.

St. Andrew's church, on an elevated site on the edge of the village of Weaverthorpe, is of an interesting and unusual appearance. Its early Norman tower, described by Nikolaus Pevsner as 'of the tall slim Northumberland type', has a rounded projection which houses the staircase, and gives it the air of a fortified tower. In the porch above the doorway a square sundial bears the Latin inscription *Herbertus Wintonie hoc monasterium fecit* (Herbert of Winchester built this church) which has made it possible to date its founding to the early 12th century. Inside is a Norman tub font with a carved pattern covering its surface, and the unusual feature, above the high tower arch, of a doorway.

A large statue of St. Andrew dominates one side of the Chancel arch and the pulpit at the other side is of an unusual design in wrought iron, looking rather like a small period house balcony. Both these features date from its restoration - like so many East Yorkshire churches - by Sir Tatton Sykes in the late 1800s.

Outside the porch lies a very weathered effigy. On the opposite side of the path a large squat column on a stepped base, with a square depression in the top, was a puzzle to me. It bore no inscriptions and looked as if something had once been attached at the top, but I was unable to solve the mystery of its purpose. Perhaps someone could tell me?

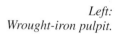

Left:
Wrought-iron pulpit.

Below:
A strange object.

Left:
St. Andrew's church.

Photos by
Eileen Rennison.

52. WELTON

Dick Turpin's Arrest.

Welton is off the A63(T) about 9 miles west of Hull. The Green Dragon is in Cowgate, to the right before the green and across from the church.

Dick Turpin was not the romantic figure that he is often portrayed, but a cattle and horse stealer, a highway robber, a common thief and a drunkard. His legendary ride to York on his horse Black Bess never actually took place, though he did flee to Yorkshire after accidentally shooting a companion in Whitechapel, London. Calling himself John Palmer he settled in the lovely village of Welton as a gentleman horse-dealer - in reality selling stolen horses. This disguise he might well have maintained had it not been for his violent temper and propensity for drink. In a drunken brawl he shot a neighbour's prize cock and though he tried to escape by jumping through a window he was arrested in the Green Dragon inn and taken in custody to York. In the course of inquiries his many felonies came to light and there on 7th April 1739 he was executed on the gallows. A plaque in the Green Dragon tells his story. In the churchyard an epitaph teases us with another story, leaving the details to our imagination. In 1719, one, Jeremiah Found, died aged eighty-four, having had no less than eight wives. A record to beat even today's film-stars surely, and one which leaves us wanting to know more about both the man and the wives.

The Green Dragon.
Photo by Richard Hebblethwaite.

53. WHITBY

Whitby is about 20 miles north of Scarborough on the A171. St. Mary's Church is on the East Cliff, over Bridge Street and through the pedestrianised area to the Church Stairs.

To reach it by car turn right after Bridge Street along Church Street, then left into Green Lane and left again along Abbey Lane. There is parking on the cliff top.

The Church Up Stairs.

St. Mary's Church stands with the Abbey ruins, exposed to the elements, high above the sea on the eroding edge of the East Cliff, reached from as early as 1370 by a stairway. Between 1750 and 1770 the wooden stairs were replaced by stone, and although the number of them has varied over the years, since the 1830s the visitors counting as they climb have found them to be 199. A yearly event was a race up and down the steps, which when it was revived in 1977 was won in 32 seconds; a fact which may leave the slow, already panting climber in need of a 'sit-down' on the benches placed on the flat areas found at intervals along the steps. These appropriate resting points were originally much needed coffin rests for the bearers carrying those on their last journey up to the church. The climb is not for the frail or the unfit, but for others, on reaching the top it is well worth the effort.

The Church Below Decks.

The exterior of St. Mary's Church in no way prepares one for its unusual interior; a fascinating jumble of galleries pillars and high box-pews. The pulpit dating from 1778 is an elaborate three-decker, the lower deck for the use of the parish clerk the next

for the priest taking the service, and the top for the preaching of the sermon. A vicar in the early nineteenth century installed the unusual sound amplifying tubes attached to it, so that his deaf wife might be sure of hearing his every word. Behind the pulpit is one of the few remaining so-called 'jade's 'pews, reserved for the public humiliation before the congregation, of a woman guilty of adultery. Barefooted and dressed in a sort of shroud, she was made to walk to the pew, there to listen to a sermon directed specifically to her, calling for her to repent. No suggestion we notice that it takes two!

Two thousand people can be seated in the church, with pews once owned and reserved by various people, others for the use of 'Strangers only'. The most comfortable pew, crossing the Chancel Arch on 'barley sugar' columns, dates from about 1620. Built for Sir Hugh Cholmley, Lord of the Manor of Whitby, it boasts its own private entry with a flight of stairs from outside.

The Cholmley pew and private entrance.

But to fully appreciate the particular individuality and character of the church one must raise one's eyes to the roof and clerestorey. In the 17th century, when the roof needed replacing, the local ship's carpenters were called in to do the work, and not surprisingly the result resembled the deck of a ship, to which the rows of ship's cabin windows were later added. With a little imagination one can sit in the church and feel that one is below decks on an old sailing ship. What could be more appropriate for Whitby with its shipbuilding and seagoing traditions?

Pagan Temple in a Christian Church.

Among the many interesting things in St. Mary's church is a miniature Greek temple in the porch, an unusual memorial to the lifeboatmen lost in the great disaster of February 9th 1861. Five vessels had been grounded in appalling weather, and five successful rescues had been effected when a sixth vessel went aground. In gale-force winds, mountainous waves and driving snow and sleet the lifeboat set out once again but capsized. Several thousand people watched helplessly as the crew were lost. Only one man, Henry Freeman, was saved; the only man wearing the cork life-jacket which had been newly introduced. It may seem a strange memorial for such a tragic and poignant event. Quite simply the minister had seen it in a shop in Marylebone, liked it and brought it back to Whitby; a pagan temple in a christian church to commemorate a group of brave men. Another interesting memorial can be found in a niche in the outside wall of the church beside the Cholmley pew entrance. Francis and Mary Huntrodd had the distinction of being born on the same day September 19th 1600, married on their birthday,

brought up a family of twelve children and died aged 80 on their birthday, within five hours of each other. As their gravestone puts it -
'So fit a match surely could never be,
Both in their lives and in their deaths agree.'

A Strange Phenomenon.

Whitby and Scarborough are both situated only 20 miles apart on the east coast, yet Scarborough's cliffs are North and South while Whitby has an East Cliff and a West Cliff, a difference accounted for by Whitby's northern orientation. Because of this it is possible from Whitby to see the strange phenomenon, during two weeks before and after the summer solstice on 21st June, of the sun both rising and setting over the sea.

Caedmon's Cross.

An impressive sight as it stands at the top of the Church Stairs, overlooking the town and sea towards the West Cliff, is the cross commemorating Caedmon, the humble 7th century herdsman of Whitby Abbey, who, through a vision, found his voice as a poet of sacred verses and songs. The cross was erected in 1898 but its design is based on the 7th century cross at Ruthwell on the Solway Firth.

54. WITHERNSEA

Withernsea is on the coast about 17 miles south of Hornsea on the B1242 or a similar distance from Hull on the A1033.

The Lighthouse is open weekends March - October from 1 to 5pm and weekdays July - August - mid September from 11am to 5pm.

A Gateway to the Sea and an Inland Light.

Withernsea is an ancient town mentioned in the Domesday Book, but it was the coming of the railway in Victorian times that led to its development as a seaside resort. Among other improvements and attractions a pier almost 2000 feet long was built, only to be destroyed in October 1880, by a ship driven into it by a storm. Today, what may look like a mock castle, is in fact its castellated gateway, all that remains of an ambitious scheme but still an unusual and prominent feature of the promenade.

Withernsea is also unusual in that its lighthouse stands, not as one might expect, out to sea or on a promontory but in the main street among the houses. It ceased its function in 1976 and is today a museum of local history and the Royal National Lifeboat Institute. It was bought by the sister of the actress Kay Kendal, who starred in the classic comedy *Genevieve*, made in 1954 about the London to Brighton Veteran Car Race. Their grandfather had been involved in the building of the lighthouse and

was also the last coxswain of the local deep-sea lifeboat. It now serves as a memorial to the Withernsea-born actress who died so tragically young.

A gateway out to sea.
Photo by Richard Hebblethwaite.

itself can still be seen in the Natural History Museum in London.

55. WOLD NEWTON

Remembering a Meteorite.

From Bridlington take the A165 for about a mile, then turn left to Burton Fleming (about 6 miles); approximately $1\frac{1}{2}$ miles beyond the village turn right for $\frac{1}{3}$ mile then left into

Wold Newton about 1 mile. At the crossroads in the village turn left for Thwing and Wold Cottage and the monument, both off to the right.

One day in 1795 the quiet village of Wold Newton was disturbed and excited by the arrival of a huge meteorite falling from the skies. It fell a short distance from Wold Cottage, the home of magistrate, Mr. Edward Topham, who immediately took charge, having it dug out and measured. A yard long and twenty-eight inches across and weighing 56 lbs, it needed several men to remove it from the ground. The outside was black and glassy smooth, while the inside was white and of a granular structure. It was sent to London where it was examined and analysed by scientists, who up to that time had poured scorn on stories of stones falling from the sky. Edward Topham felt that such an unusual event should also have a lasting memorial where the meteorite actually fell, and as a result of his interest and initiative an obelisk now stands on that exact spot. Its location is visible across the fields but it is on private land and should anyone wish to view it more closely this can only be done with the permission of the owners at the farm. The meteorite

Remembering a meteorite.
Photo by Richard Hebblethwaite.